PAPERS ON
SHELLEY
WORDSWORTH
& OTHERS

PAPERS ON
SHELLEY
WORDSWORTH
& OTHERS

By

J. A. CHAPMAN

Essay Index Reprint Series

BOOKS FOR LIBRARIES PRESS
FREEPORT, NEW YORK

First Published 1929

First Reprinting in this Series 1967

Second Reprinting 1969

STANDARD BOOK NUMBER:

8369-0288-2

LIBRARY OF CONGRESS CATALOG CARD NUMBER:

67-23191

PRINTED IN THE UNITED STATES OF AMERICA

ACKNOWLEDGEMENT

TWO of the papers in this book were published in the *Calcutta Review* and five of them in *The Englishman*. I have to thank the Editors for the courtesy of their permission to republish the matter. The papers have all of them been rewritten.

CONTENTS

Shelley and Francis Thompson . 1

Wordsworth 19

Coleridge 39

Poetry and Experience . . . 53

The Greatest Poetry . . . 76

The Future of English Poetry . . 88

Dr. Saintsbury's Heresy . . . 103

Walt Whitman 115

Richard Middleton . . . 128

Dr. Edward Thompson's Poetry . 136

Publishing Lyrical Poetry . . 155

In Conclusion 164

SHELLEY AND FRANCIS THOMPSON

MAN has always been liable to be tripped up by this, that he cannot rigidly distinguish between himself as a play-actor and himself in what may be called real life. It may be called that, though in a sense man's play-acting is as real as any other part of his acting. There is, however, a difference. A man will play Hamlet on the stage, and forget for the time partly, as those watching him may forget completely, that he is really Garrick and not Hamlet; but if after the play was over, he still thought himself Hamlet, people would say he was mad, and if the spectators were found the next day in the streets of London, inquiring for the house of Polonius, they would be said to be mad. Where men are not seen to be mad is when they carry over the play-acting, say, in their religion into their real lives. I perhaps ought not to say as much as that. This would be enough to say,—that if men did mix play-acting with their religion, and if they carried over some of that play-acting into their real lives, they would not be seen to be mad. It would take a sharper eye to see that than man has.

I believe that man does act other than consciously on the boards of the world, and that he does not rigidly distinguish his two parts. Disraeli did act the part of leader of the Conservative party as well as take his leadership seriously, and I do not think he always distinguished clearly between the two parts. Such a one would commit himself, in the mood of the only half-conscious play-actor, to positions in which he could not sustain himself in his hours of sober earnestness. I see all man as that figure, and much of the sin and misery in the world as due to this, that men, not to use soft words, easily lend themselves to a lie. It ought to be some one's office to call attention to the lies, so that human life might be more solidly built up. I am here going to call attention to the lie, as I cannot but see it, in that admired thing, the essay of Francis Thompson on Shelley.

I have heard the essay spoken of as the best in the language. That it cannot be; for in a sense there is no such thing as the essay, as in a sense there is no such thing as the poem. There are epic poems, narrative poems, lyrical poems, and so on. So there are many short prose writings that, because there is no other generic term to call them by, are called essays; but they are of so diverse kinds, that there is no comparing them. You cannot compare things as dissimilar as Addison's accounts of Sir Roger and Will Honeycomb, Lamb's *Dissertation upon Roast Pig*, Hazlitt's *Indian Jugglers*, Macaulay's *Milton*, Carlyle's *Diamond Necklace*, De Quincey's *Bentley*, and Thompson's *Shelley*.

Of its kind—that is, literary criticism—I do not think I regard Thompson's essay as the best. There are essays of that kind of Arnold's that I rank much higher, but I may rank those essays higher than any one else does. Thompson's essay contains no words that more fully reveal what poetry is, and it is disfigured by repeated excesses. There was apparently something in his dealing with a poet whose work is remarkable for its wealth of imagery, which wealth, however, was exaggerated in Thompson's mind, that urged Thompson, another poet whose work is remarkable for wealth of imagery, to over-indulge in decoration. His description of Mrs. Browning as 'a fair-coined soul that lay rusting in a pool of tears' has something of that excess in it that would make any one who should read the context aloud slightly shiver. There is excess in:

'The lark that is the gossip of heaven, the winds that pluck the grey from the beards of the billows, the clouds that are snorted from the sea's broad nostril, all the elemental spirits of Nature, take from his verse perpetual

incarnation and reincarnation, pass in a thousand glorious
transmigrations through the radiant forms of his imagery.'

That would have been better, if there had been
a little less of it: it begins to weaken with the
adjective before 'nostril', and thence to the end it
gets steadily weaker.

Again in

'No trappings are too splendid for the swift steeds of
sunrise. His sword-hilt may be rough with jewels, but
it is the hilt of an Excalibur. His thoughts scorch through
all the folds of expression. His cloth of gold bursts at the
flexures, and shows the naked poetry,'

and in

'The coldest moon of an idea rises haloed through his
vaporous imagination. The dimmest-sparked chip of a
conception blazes and scintillates in the subtile oxygen
of his mind. The most wrinkled Aeson of an abstruseness
leaps rosy out of his bubbling genius;'

—in those there is an excess that defeats the
writer's aim, which is to convey a meaning about
Shelley that others might put to their use. No
meaning is clearly conveyed; for the mind is cap-
tured by Thompson's sound, and enmeshed in his
imagery. If a thing is to make a lasting impression,
it must be such as this—Arnold is speaking of
Keats and Maurice de Guérin—'when they speak
of the world they speak like Adam naming by
divine inspiration the creatures; their expression

corresponds with the thing's essential reality'. A man can carry that in his head: it will come back to him when he reads:

> Sometimes whoever seeks abroad may find
> Thee sitting careless on a granary floor,
> Thy hair soft-lifted by the winnowing wind,

and will know better in what inspired world his footsteps lead him.

Even the gorgeous

'The universe is his box of toys. He dabbles his fingers in the day-fall. He is gold-dusty with tumbling amidst the stars. He makes bright mischief with the moon. The meteors nuzzle their noses in his hand' . . .

even that goes on too long, and the concluding words, which one cannot but see that Sir Thomas Browne would have known better than to write—'to see how she will look nicest in her song'—are feeble.

It is none the less, and even though excess is not its only grave fault, which it is not, a great piece of writing. It begins well (where it does really begin: the appeal to the Church on behalf of poetry the rest of us may ignore) with: 'We have among us no lineal descendant, in the poetical order, of Shelley.' Not one? Not Thompson himself? One thinks he must have known that, if there was no lineal descendant, there was a man, himself, that came very near to being one.

What follows is good too—the examination of the tyranny of the 'poetic diction' that had succeeded, even after Wordsworth's freeing of the English race, to the old bad one of the time of Pope and his successors;—the tyranny of the 'felicitous phrase' that Tennyson abused; but even in that part of the essay there is something wrong —a note of unwarranted pessimism. Nothing is worse than to disseminate pessimism among poets. After saying that the literary revolution against the despotic diction of Pope seemed issuing in a despotism of its own making, he adds: 'We are self-conscious to the finger-tips; and this inherent quality, entailing on our poetry the inevitable loss of spontaneity, ensures that whatever poets, of whatever excellence, may be born to us from the Shelleian stock, its founder's spirit can take among us no reincarnation.' Now, however certain it may be that all but the greatest spirits catch the infection of their time, and are, but in a different sense from Shakespeare's, 'subdued to what they work in, like the dyer's hand' (and perhaps in Shakespeare's sense also)—however true it may be, though strange, that men are hemmed in by their own time, and cannot win to live in a larger, it is not true that the great poet, of the greatest excellence, would not break the bonds; and there

was Browning alive in Thompson's day to prove
it in some measure. It might be proved in a
greater. To say that a 'spirit can take among us
no reincarnation' is the last thing that any leader
should say, and Thompson aimed, very rightly, at
leadership. For a man to say that he and his contemporaries must be subdued to an influence that
they themselves know to be bad—what possesses
men to think such things?

If Thompson felt as he wrote the words, as one
feels sure that he did, that he was himself as near
a lineal descendant of Shelley as there could be, he
must also have felt, as he went on to describe
Shelley—his remaining a child in the good sense
of retaining the spontaneity of childhood, and not
in the bad sense of being childish; the effect of
the persecution of his boyhood—that he was de-
scribing himself and his lot. Those are the pages
that are pathetic: one aches not to have been the
editor of that Dublin journal to whom the essay
was sent; to have been he, with all our later knowledge of Thompson and his suffering, that at least
he might have had that article accepted.

I have said that Thompson exaggerated the
wealth of imagery in Shelley's poetry. This, too,
must be emphasized. If we are to learn the most
that can be learned from any poet's work, we must

know it as it is. We must not be put off with a wrong impression.

'For astounding figurative opulence,' Thompson writes, 'Shelley yields only to Shakespeare, and even to Shakespeare not in absolute fecundity but in range of images. . . . It would have been as conscious an effort for him to speak without figure as it is for most men to speak with figure.' Again he says: 'The Metaphysical School, like Shelley, loved imagery for its own sake: and how beautiful a thing the frank toying with imagery may be, let *The Skylark* and *The Cloud* witness. It is only evil when the poet, on the straight way to a fixed object, lags continually from the path to play. This is commendable neither in poet nor errand-boy.'

In that one of Wordsworth's poems to the daisy (there are two others), the beginning of which is 'With little here to do or see,' there is what one may call 'toying with imagery'; there is:

> Many a fond and idle name
> I give to thee, for praise or blame,
> As is the humour of the game,
> 　　While I am gazing.

> A nun demure, of lowly port;
> Or sprightly maiden, of Love's court,
> In thy simplicity the sport
> 　　Of all temptations;

A queen in crown of rubies drest;
A starveling in a scanty vest;
Are all, as seems to suit thee best,
    Thy appellations.
A little Cyclops, with one eye
Staring to threaten and defy,
That thought comes next—and instantly
    The freak is over,
The shape will vanish, and behold!
A silver shield with boss of gold . . .

and so to the end. Earlier in the poem is:

I sit and play with similes,
Loose types of things through all degrees,
    Thoughts of thy raising.

That is playing with imagery, as it is natural
that a poet in a holiday mood should play; but it
is not in such moods that great poetry is written,
and that is not a great poem. It is a poem of the
fancy, and not of the imagination, to use Wordsworth's own divisions. It is significant that Arnold
did not include it in his Selection. It is true it is
in the *Golden Treasury*. Palgrave had not quite
Arnold's judgement.

I have two things to object against Thompson.
The first is that in those poems of Shelley's that he
praises highest—*The Skylark, The Cloud, The Sensitive Plant*,—there is much imagery that, if it is not
toyed with, or not as frankly as Wordsworth's toying

in that holiday mood, lacks something of the imaginative beauty that graces other Shelleian imagery. The second thing I have to object is that perhaps still more beautiful poems of Shelley's, the most beautiful of them all, it may be, are bare of imagery (that is, as bare as poetry ever can be): and, if that is so, it is simply not true that it would have been as conscious an effort for Shelley to speak without figure as it is for most men to speak with figure. Anything not true said of a master poet must be contradicted; for it is to them that we go to school.

Let us examine *To a Skylark*. In such verses, and they are of the best in the poem, as:

> Hail to thee, blithe Spirit!
>   Bird thou never wert,
> That from heaven, or near it,
>   Pourest thy full heart
> In profuse strains of unpremeditated art.
>
> The pale purple even
>   Melts around thy flight;
> Like a star of heaven
>   In the broad daylight
> Thou art unseen, but yet I hear thy shrill delight.
>
> All the earth and air
>   With thy voice is loud,
> As when night is bare,
>   From one lonely cloud
> The moon rains out her beams, and heaven is overflow'd.

> What thou art we know not;
>   What is most like thee?
> From rainbow clouds there flow not
>   Drops so bright to see
> As from thy presence showers a rain of melody—

there is very little imagery. The imagery begins
with the next verse, the playing with it, and is
continued in the four that follow; but to my mind
those five fall below the level of what has preceded,
and the sweep of the poem is not resumed until
the playing is finished, and we come again to
lines that are comparatively imagery-free; such
verses as:

> Teach us, sprite or bird,
>   What sweet thoughts are thine:
> I have never heard
>   Praise of love or wine
> That panted forth a flood of rapture so divine.

The likening of the skylark's song to the sing-
ing of a poet hidden in the light of thought, to a
high-born maiden soothing her love-laden soul in
secret hour, to a glow-worm, to a rose embowered,
to sound of vernal showers on twinkling grass—
—those do not for me reveal the secret of the
appeal of the bird's song; they are too much the
expression of the quick, playful human intellect,
and too little the surprised utterance of the won-
dering imagination.

The verse in the poem that is by general consent the most moving is entirely without imagery; this:

> We look before and after,
>> And pine for what is not:
> Our sincerest laughter
>> With some pain is fraught;
> Our sweetest songs are those that tell of saddest thought;

but there again, alas! something has to be objected; for the sad truth—no, it is glad—is that our sweetest songs do not. Search the *Golden Treasury* for what by general consent are the sweetest songs, and you will be surprised to find how few of them are sad.

Of perhaps the most beautiful Shelleian music, and note that it is almost entirely imagery-free, read these

> Out of the day and night
> A joy has taken flight:
> Fresh spring, and summer, and winter hoar
> Move my faint heart with grief, but with delight
> No more—Oh, never more!

> He will watch from dawn to gloom
> The lake-reflected sun illume
> The yellow bees in the ivy-bloom,
> Nor heed nor see what things they be—
> But from these create he can
> Forms more real than living man,
> Nurslings of Immortality!

Sun-girt City! thou hast been
Ocean's child, and then his queen;
Now is come a darker day,
And thou soon must be his prey,
If the power that raised thee here
Hallow so thy watery bier.[1]
A less drear ruin then than now,
With thy conquest-branded brow
Stooping to the slave of slaves
From thy throne among the waves
Wilt thou be—when the sea-mew
Flies, as once before it flew,
O'er thine isles depopulate,
And all is in its ancient state,
Save where many a palace-gate
With green sea-flowers overgrown
Like a rock of ocean's own,
Topples o'er the abandoned sea
As the tides change sullenly.

Art thou pale for weariness
Of climbing heaven, and gazing on the earth,
Wandering companionless
Among the stars that have a different birth?

How calm it was! The silence there
By such a chain was bound,
That even the busy woodpecker
Made stiller with her sound
The inviolable quietness.

[1] So punctuated in my copy of the *Golden Treasury*, but should there not be a full-stop after *prey*, and only a comma after *bier*?

I could lie down like a tired child,
And weep away the life of care
Which I have borne, and yet must bear,
Till death like sleep might steal on me,
And I might feel in the warm air
My cheek grow cold, and hear the sea
Breathe o'er my dying brain its last monotony.

The fountains mingle with the river
And the rivers with the ocean,
The winds of heaven mix for ever
With a sweet emotion;
Nothing in the world is single,
All things by a law divine
In one another's being mingle—
Why not I with thine?

I fear thy kisses, gentle maiden;
Thou needest not fear mine;
My spirit is too deeply laden
Ever to burthen thine.

Those poems, I say, are little, or not at all, excellent because of their imagery, but for their straightforwardness and simplicity—or do I not understand what Thompson means by imagery?

These others are marked by wealth of imagery:

Wrap thy form in a mantle grey,
Star-inwrought;
Blind with thy hair the eyes of Day;
Kiss her until she be wearied out:

Then wander o'er city and sea and land,
Touching all with thine opiate wand—
Come, long-sought!

There grew pied wind-flowers and violets,
    Daisies, those pearled Arcturi of the earth,
The constellated flower that never sets;
    Faint oxlips; tender blue-bells, at whose birth
The sod scarce heaved; and that tall flower that wets
    Like a child, half in tenderness and mirth—
Its mother's face with heaven-collected tears,
When the low wind, its playmate's voice, it hears.

O wild West Wind, thou breath of Autumn's being,
Thou, from whose unseen presence the leaves dead
Are driven, like ghosts from an enchanter fleeing,
Yellow, and black, and pale, and hectic red,
Pestilence-stricken multitudes! O thou
Who chariotest to their dark wintry bed
The wingèd seeds, where they lie cold and low,
Each like a corpse within its grave, until
Thine azure sister of the Spring shall blow
Her clarion o'er the dreaming earth, and fill
(Driving sweet buds like flocks to feed in air)
With living hues and odours plain and hill:
Wild Spirit, which art moving everywhere;
Destroyer and Preserver; Hear, oh hear!

Thou on whose stream, 'mid the steep sky's commotion
Loose clouds like earth's decaying leaves are shed,
Shook from the tangled boughs of heaven and ocean,
Angels of rain and lightning! there are spread

On the blue surface of thine airy surge,
Like the bright hair uplifted from the head
Of some fierce Maenad, ev'n from the dim verge
Of the horizon to the zenith's height—
The locks of the approaching storm. Thou dirge
Of the dying year, to which this closing night
Will be the dome of a vast sepulchre,
Vaulted with all thy congregated might
Of vapours, from whose solid atmosphere
Black rain, and fire, and hail will burst: Oh hear!

Make me thy lyre, ev'n as the forest is;
What if my leaves are falling like its own!
The tumult of thy mighty harmonies
Will take from both a deep autumnal tone,
Sweet though in sadness. Be thou, Spirit fierce,
My spirit! be thou me, impetuous one!
Drive my dead thoughts over the universe,
Like withered leaves, to quicken a new birth;
And, by the incantation of this verse,
Scatter, as from an unextinguished hearth
Ashes and sparks, my words among mankind!
Be through my lips to unawakened earth
The trumpet of a prophecy! O wind,
If Winter comes, can Spring be far behind?

That, I have long thought, and not *To a Skylark*, or *The Cloud*, or *The Sensitive Plant*, is the
finest poem that Shelley wrote, and it comes back
to me now with interest that a man, Charles Rus-
sell, who read much poetry aloud to me, and always

what he thought the poet's best work, read *The Ode to the West Wind* aloud to me, and never read, and I think never would have read, *To a Skylark* or *Adonais*.

That is, I think, Shelley's finest poem, and it is the fullest of imagery; yet I should like to make an end of quoting, not with it, but with some words of his that are imagery-free. These lines:

> And wind-flowers and violets
> Which yet join not scent to hue
> Crown the pale year weak and new;
> When night is left behind
> In the deep east, dim and blind,
> And the blue moon is over us,
> And the multitudinous
> Billows murmur at our feet,
> Where the earth and ocean meet,
> And all things seem only one
> In the universal Sun.

Or better still, perhaps, end with this:

> Music, when soft voices die,
> Vibrates in the memory—
> Odours, when sweet violets sicken,
> Live within the sense they quicken.
> Rose leaves, when the rose is dead,
> Are heaped for the beloved's bed;
> And so thy thoughts, when Thou art gone,
> Love itself shall slumber on.

One's conclusion must be, then, that Thompson was half-consciously play-acting when he wrote his essay; that what he wrote had rather for him the value of ritual than hard truth. Much might be said as to the value of ritual in human life, and a man might deliberately determine for such a quantity of it in all his affairs; but one cannot but see that, when the supreme moments of testing come for men, as at the end of that July in 1914, all of ritual that had been built up falls to pieces. One cannot but think that the life for man that is behind the veil is to be seized only by hands strong enough to rend the veil, and that they are the hands that do not swerve from truth.

WORDSWORTH

'POETRY', wrote Wordsworth, 'is the spontaneous overflow of powerful feelings: it takes its origin from emotion recollected in tranquillity.' It certainly may do so; most, if not all of, Wordsworth's own poetry did; but that is not to say that it always does: it is not even to say that it generally does. *The Ode to the Nightingale* was for the greater part, and was perhaps entirely, the expression of the emotions and feelings of the moment: Keats and the bird were alone in the Hampstead garden. *The Ode to the Grecian Urn* was written on the evening of the day that Haydon took Keats to see the Elgin Marbles; so within a few hours of that inspired event. That Wordsworth's dictum is an erroneous one is not what interests me, however, and such is my reverence for Wordsworth, and such my concern for his fame, that could mere wishing the dictum to be true make it so, forthwith I would wish it true, though that would make what I have written myself, and have thought was poetry, be not poetry; for hardly a line of it expresses emotion recollected in tranquillity. My interest is to call attention to the fact that, though not true, the dictum is yet put forward with all

that air of being beyond contradiction, and to
draw from that a conclusion about Wordsworth.

Again Wordsworth says, to give the argument
in Professor Garrod's summary of it (that will save
time; it will also make for clearness): 'Nature has
safeguarded for the creative artist a "state of enjoyment" in the act of creating; and he owes it to his
readers to communicate to them this "over-balance
of pleasure". A principal means of doing so con-
sists in the use of "the music of harmonious metrical language". "Painful feeling" is "always found
intermingled with powerful descriptions of the
deeper passions"; and the description of such
passions is the more powerful when conveyed in
"language closely resembling that of real life".
Yet in the circumstance of metre the language of
poetry will "differ so widely from real life as to
create an indistinct perception", to "throw a sort of
half-consciousness of unsubstantial existence over
the whole composition".'

Wordsworth, in the writing (the Preface to
Lyrical Ballads) in which the argument so sum-
marized occurs, is contending against the use
of the outworn poetic diction of the successors
to Pope. The giving up of poetic diction would
involve, he thought, the giving up of metre also,

unless reason could be shown why it should not
be given up although the other was. Metre must be
retained—this is the argument—because poetry
written in the language of real life would be too
harrowing without metre.

At this much later stage, after so much more
thought about the matter, we should think it
reason enough to give for abandoning poetic diction that that diction is dead, and cannot be used
for the expression of anything not equally dead
and stark and wooden. A man taking that simple
view, would see that there was no need to say
anything about the language that should be used
instead of poetic diction, as that it must be language closely resembling that of real life—a saying
that gives an opening to much obvious criticism.
My life is as real as my nearest neighbour's at
this moment (he is the caretaker of the building
in which I am at work), but my language is very
unlike his.

Any simple, seeing mind (I maintain that a
mind can be both simple and seeing, while ready,
of course, to admit that most simple minds see
nothing to the point in such a matter as mine),
which had seen that poetic diction must be given
up for the dead thing it is, would have seen an end
there. He would not have seen the giving up of

a dead idiom as involving the giving up of metre.
He would have had it in his memory that metre
has been used since the beginning of time, and
that there is nothing more alive. That Wordsworth, who had not seen poetic diction simply as
dead, should have seen the giving up of metre as
involved in the giving up of the diction, unless he
could give a reason why it should not be given up,
notwithstanding—that cannot just be dismissed.
It is essential to my argument that I should examine the matter.

Assume, then, some one's question, Wordsworth's own, in fact: 'Must not metre be given
up also?' Wordsworth answers the question with
the same air of delivering a truth as he showed in
the dictum about what it is in which poetry has its
origin, but to my mind with as little success in
explaining anything; and it is nothing to the point,
as against me, that I have shown that there was
really nothing that had to be explained; for the
matter now is that Wordsworth, seeing something
to explain, explained it as he did.

If painful feeling is always found intermingled
with powerful descriptions of the deeper passions,
and if the use of metre (so that an indistinct perception be created) is to render what would be
painful not so, then a great deal of great poetry

does not deal with the deeper passions. Such
poetry as the following does not:

> Some say that ever 'gainst that season comes
> Wherein our Saviour's birth is celebrated,
> The bird of dawning singeth all night long:
> And then, they say, no spirit can walk abroad;
> The nights are wholesome; then no planets strike,
> No fairy takes, nor witch hath power to charm,
> So hallow'd and so gracious is the time.

Put up your bright swords or the dew will rust them.

> If it were now to die,
> 'Twere now to be most happy; for I fear,
> My soul hath her content so absolute
> That not another comfort like to this
> Succeeds in unknown fate.

> unheard
> Save by the quiet primrose, and the span
> Of heaven and few ears.

To say that there is painful feeling in the passion
of those, or that there would have been, but that
the metre creates an indistinct perception, is to
say that which is not true. In Shakespeare's or in
Keats's prose (what beautiful prose it would have
been!) there would have been no painful feeling.
Neither is there, the sense being expressed as
poetry, in metre, any indistinctness of perception.
The sense is as clear as bright flowers are in sunshine.

Even in:

> Absent thee from felicity awhile,
> And in this harsh world draw thy breath in pain
> To tell my story;

and

> Vex not his ghost: O, let him pass: he hates him
> That would upon the rack of this rough world
> Stretch him out longer;

if there is painful feeling, it is still there for all the metre.

My purpose, however, is not so much to contest Wordsworth's argument, as to call attention to the fact that it was put forward just as if, though the truth in such a vexed question as how men came to use metre, and what the use adds to poetry, is hard to win, everything was quite clear to him. There is no faltering in his phrases. There must be indistinctness of perception, he says in effect, and that is what metre gives; the truth being that there need be no indistinctness of perception; there never is in great poetry; metre would not give it.

What kind of mind had this theorizing man? with what kind of mind did he begin? Begin, not as poet, be it understood, but as thinker and reasoner.

For a full answer to my question I refer you to Professor Garrod's *Wordsworth*. From it you will learn that Wordsworth was influenced, even

at times dominated, by contemporaries—Erasmus
Darwin, Rousseau, Beaupuy, and Godwin. By
these when he was a young man, later by Coleridge and Dorothy Wordsworth, and in his old age,
Professor Garrod says, 'he drugged himself with
the humdrum of political and social and religious
orthodoxy'. The only mention in the story of any
influence not being that of a contemporary is the
influence of Spinoza, and Spinoza's influence on
Wordsworth, we are told, was short-lived. In my
own mind I compare Wordsworth's mind with
that of a contemporary of my own, and then I am
struck by the absence in Wordsworth's case of any
effective sense, at any time of his life, of ours being
a very old world, a long succession of generations,
the last of which, at any comparatively late point of
historical time, could not reasonably hope to do
more than add a little to the accumulated wisdom.
It is to be expected that Jack Brown's thought-
world and Tom Robinson's should be found to
begin not long before their birth. It is to be hoped
that the thought-world of any one claiming the
right to instruct mankind should not begin then.
Such a one ought to be found to have more sense
than to allow himself to be greatly influenced, let
alone to be dominated, by any contemporary
Godwin. He should not be heard saying to a

student of the Temple, as Wordsworth once was:
'Throw aside your books of chemistry, and read
Godwin upon Necessity.' Books of chemistry are
to be thrown aside for nothing less than Aristotle
and Plato, the Bible, Dante, Shakespeare, and
such-like books.

I should, then, be put in the frame of mind of the
man who would be apt to approach any theorizing
of Wordsworth's (not for nothing did FitzGerald
always call him Daddy Wordsworth) half-prepared
to find it of no very great importance. He was
a great poet, I should say, and was also given to
theorizing about poetry; but it remains to be
proved that he theorized with the same 'mind' with
which he wrote his verse, and that his theory is
as good as his poetry. But, says Professor Garrod,
his poetry becomes fully intelligible only in the
light of his theorizing. If you reject the theory,
you shut yourself out from full understanding of
the poetry. Perhaps, yet it may be that it is not
so; it may be that full understanding, or, as I should
prefer to put it, full enjoyment, is not to be reached
in any light but that of an equally gifted poetic
soul. For other people, I would venture to assume,
the fullest understanding and enjoyment possible
is to be gained less by their grappling with the
difficulties presented by the theorizing than by
constant reading of the poetry.

What Wordsworth may exactly have meant in this or that passage may no doubt be more clearly grasped in the light of his theory; but if the meaning of words is a poor meaning, in correspondence with a muddled theory, those words cannot have a high value as poetry; and so, if one did not quite know what they meant, it would not so much matter. There is a great deal of poetry that men can afford to ignore. In any case it is better to fail of complete understanding of any man's poetry than to make any concession to the so human inclination to believe some lies; even if the lies are about the origin of a man's, any man's, body of poetry, or the virtue of metre. Whatever is the true theory of poetry, one might be so extravagant as to think, *le bon Dieu* will look after it, and keep it for us.

True, it is a great theme, even the greatest; for in the light in which the theory of poetry, or the soul of poetry, should be fully understood, the nature of man would be fully understood also, and the nature of the universe in which he finds himself; but it is not to be expected, surely, that what any man may have to say at so late a date as Wordsworth's would add much to the words of Jesus and others of old time except for those by whom are clearly heard only the trumpet-calls of the men

who stand near them in time; that is to say, the
mass of mankind. The mass of mankind has not
advanced far in growth towards the fullness of the
stature of Christ (in whatever sense, not for any
man to lay down, those words are to be understood).
It is that fullness of stature to which all men should
endeavour to grow, keeping steadily before them
the conditions in which such growth is possible,
and that it alone of all things matters; that it is
men's greatest concern. But that by the way. To
return to Wordsworth's poetry.

Grant that there may be a great value for the
understanding of Wordsworth's poetry in an
understanding of his theorizing, but attend most
to such of the theory as is embodied in the poetry
itself, to such as:

> those first affections,
> Those shadowy recollections,
> Which, be they what they may,
> Are yet the fountain-light of all our day,
> Are yet a master-light of all our seeing,

and, as our seeing (in that all-embracing sense) is
our poetry, are also the master-light of it.

Attend to such as:

> the light of sense
> Goes out, but with a flash that has revealed
> The invisible world;

and

> Nor less I deem that there are Powers
>   Which of themselves our minds impress;
> That we can feed this mind of ours
>   In a wise passiveness.

That is what Wordsworth did, to put it so; he 'lit' the light of sense, and in his poetry he expressed the invisible world, the particular aspect of it, that the flash had revealed to him; and he 'lit' the light of sense (it sounds a contradiction, perhaps) while remaining wisely passive.

If those utterances of Wordsworth constitute theory, it may be objected, ours is a deeply twilight world. Well, what then? Wordsworth's poetry, after all, may be—I do not say that it must be, for I accept it from Professor Garrod that for him Wordsworth's poetry would be much less intelligible without Wordsworth's theory—but only that it may be fully enjoyed without any theory. It may be by those who enjoy poetry with one 'mind' and theorize with another, which is just as possible as that men should write poetry with one 'mind' and theorize with another, and that I know for certain as a thing that can be and has been.

The Wordsworth addition of wealth in my own emotional life—it is of that that I would speak now. Writing (that means committing oneself) as one hardly sufficiently prepared to write, I should say that Wordsworth never comes near Keats in revealing what it is in Nature that man specially hears the call of, and is specially moved by; what thrills him;—that there is nothing in the whole body of Wordsworth's poetry equal in the power of revelation to:

> Sometimes whoever seeks abroad may find
> Thee sitting careless on a granary floor,
> Thy hair soft-lifted by the winnowing wind;

or, to pass from Keats to Shelley, equal in power of revelation to:

> Wrap thy form in a mantle grey,
> Star-inwrought!
> Blind with thine hair the eyes of day,

but then such utterances contain for me almost the whole possible range of Nature poetry, just as I cannot conceive of anything more charged with all the poetry of speech than:

> the fleecy star that bears
> Andromeda far off Atlantic seas.

Wordsworth is far too easily content, and it explains also, I think, his childishness as a theoriser—he is far too easily content with such lines as:

> And O ye Fountains, Meadows, Hills, and Groves.

There was a time when meadow, grove, and stream,
The earth, and every common sight,
To me did seem
Apparelled in celestial light,
The glory and the freshness of a dream.

    ·   ·   ·   ·   ·

The rainbow comes and goes,
And lovely is the rose;
The moon doth with delight
Look round her when the heavens are bare;
Waters on a starry night
Are beautiful and fair;
The sunshine is a glorious birth;

which are all more of the nature of inventory or catalogue than poetry has any right to be.

Therefore am I still
A lover of the meadows and the woods,
And mountains.

    ·   ·   ·   ·   ·

after many wanderings, many years
Of absence, these steep woods and lofty cliffs,
And this green pastoral landscape . . .

There is so much of that kind of inventory or catalogue writing in Wordsworth, and such writing is a turning away from the great difficulty of expression. An inventory, which any child is master of, expresses nothing. One has the sense of the beauty of the countryside in autumn; one has that sense so fully in one's heart that

it is a burden: Keats speaks out of his divine
mouth:

Thy hair soft-lifted by the winnowing wind,

and the burden is gone; for it has been expressed.
Wordsworth's catalogues leave one quite un-
moved, or moved to boredom.

Of such of Wordworth's poetry as speaks of
Nature, man being absent (there is no Nature
known to man, of course, from which his mind is
entirely absent), the most moving that I can
immediately call to memory, and I have not time
to search the whole book for better examples, if
there be any better, are passages in *The Prelude*
and *The Leech-gatherer*. Wordsworth and his two
brothers went out to watch for the coming of the
led palfreys on which they should ride home at
the beginning of one of their school vacations. He
watched, half-sheltered by a naked wall, with a
sheep couched on one hand and a blasted hawthorn
standing on the other. Before they had been ten
days at home their father died, and the event
appeared to Wordsworth's mind a chastisement
for his impatience to see the palfreys come into
sight, he being fortunate in this, one might think,
that he could think of nothing worse to be chas-
tised for. He tells us all this in a passage at the
end of Book XII, a passage, if I remember rightly

that I was directed to by De Quincey first of all
(anything that he should say upon such a matter
would be well worth reading), and then Wordsworth goes on:

> afterwards, the wind and sleety rain,
> And all the business of the elements,
> The single sheep, and the one blasted tree,
> And the bleak music from that old stone wall,
> The noise of wood and water, and the mist . . .

but at that point, unfortunately, the writing drops
to commonplace again. The lines I have quoted
have haunted me for above a quarter of a century,
—and yet it may be noted that the form is still
that of inventory or catalogue.

Then there is the passage in *The Prelude* in which
Wordsworth, who had stealthily rowed across to
the opposite, lonelier, side of a lake, is made by
a sudden pan-fear to row quickly back, tells how
the mountains that rose one by one into view
seemed living things that were moving after him.

It is not a passage in *The Leech-gatherer* so much
as the whole poem, or, if it is a passage, it is this
one, in which a man figures, it is true, but not his
mind, only his shape:

> While he was talking thus, the lonely place,
> The old man's shape, and speech—all troubled me:
> In my mind's eye I seemed to see him pace

Wordsworth

About the weary moors continually,
Wandering about alone and silently.

    .   .   .   .   .

As a huge stone is sometimes seen to lie
Couched on the bald top of an eminence;
Wonder to all who do the same espy,
By what means it could thither come, and whence;
So that it seems a thing endued with sense:
Like a sea-beast crawled forth, that on a shelf
Of rock or sand reposeth, there to sun itself;
Such seemed this man.

But, as I have said, it is rather the whole poem.

The greatest of Wordsworth to me is the body of poetry that has for its subject the mind of man, the divinely made cup out of which pour his love and desire, and in which gathers his peace; or, not to circumscribe the theme too narrowly, the mind and destiny of man. This is the theme, though the things spoken of are predominantly natural objects of Shakespeare's:

That time of year thou mayst in me behold,
When yellow leaves, or none, or few do hang
Against those boughs that shake against the cold.

    .   .   .   .   .   .

Like as the waves make towards the pebbled shore,
So do our minutes hasten to their end.

It is the theme also of Wordsworth's

A Maid whom there were none to praise
And very few to love; . . .

> A violet by a mossy stone
>   Half hidden from the eye!
> Fair as a star, when only one
>   Is shining in the sky.

∴

Dear Child! dear Girl! that walkest with me here,
If thou appear untouched by solemn thought,
Thy nature is not therefore less divine.

∴

> She was . . .
> A lovely apparition, sent
> To be a moment's ornament;
> Her eyes as stars of twilight fair;
> Like twilight's, too, her dusky hair;
> But all things else about her drawn
> From May-time . . .

to give those first, as descriptions of the most delicate and the most adored part of mankind—mankind expressed as girlhood—and described by Wordsworth, surely, with a more complete surrender to its inexpressible beauty than any other man had made. Then, the theme being ever more strictly man, such passages as:

> There are who ask not if thine eye
> Be on them; who, in love and truth,
> Where no misgiving is, rely
> Upon the genial sense of youth;
> Glad hearts! without reproach or blot;
> Who do thy work, and know it not.

.   .   .

Serene will be our days and bright,
And happy will our nature be,
When love is an unerring light,
And joy its own security.

Not for these I raise
The song of thanks and praise;
But for those obstinate questionings
Of sense and outward things,
Fallings from us, vanishings;
Blank misgivings of a Creature
Moving about in worlds not realized,
High instincts before which our mortal Nature
Did tremble like a guilty thing surprised:
But for those first affections,
Those shadowy recollections,
Which, be they what they may,
Are yet the fountain-light of all our day,
Are yet a master-light of all our seeing;
Uphold us, cherish, and have power to make
Our noisy years seem moments in the being
Of the eternal Silence.

The days gone by
Return upon me almost from the dawn
Of life: the hiding-places of man's power
Open.

In such strength
Of usurpation, when the light of sense
Goes out, but with a flash that has revealed
The invisible world, doth greatness make abode,

There harbours; whether we be young or old,
Our destiny, our being's heart and home,
Is with infinitude, and only there,
With hope it is, hope that can never die,
Effort and expectation and desire,
And something evermore about to be.

Who else had written of man in such words among English poets? and if it was desired that there should be later words (later words, as nearer us and expressing more our own thoughts, and in our way, or nearer it, will always have their additional, or at least their different power over us; but they should not have too much power: we are all too much tempted to lay aside the old books for new ones)—if it was desired that there should be later words to set beside:

'If ye had known me, ye should have known my Father also; and from henceforth ye know him and have seen him.   ∴

' . . . another Comforter, that he may abide with you for ever; even the Spirit of truth; whom the world cannot receive, because it seeth him not, neither knoweth him: but ye know him; for he dwelleth with you, and shall be in you—'

if words were desired to add to those, what better in the whole body of English poetry than the most inspired of Wordsworth's utterances concerning

man; of such as have been given above, and such
as the following:

> thou hast great allies;
> Thy friends are exultations, agonies,
> And love, and man's unconquerable mind.

> .   .   .   .   .

> Enough, if something from our hands have power
> To live, and act, and serve the future hour;
> And if, as towards the silent tomb we go,
> Through love, through hope, and faith's transcendent
>   dower,
> We feel that we are greater than we know.

May it not, too, be asked in conclusion, sup-
posing it to be true that without an understanding
of Wordsworth's theorizing those passages cannot
be fully understood, whether they cannot be sufficiently understood for life as a thing that men have
to live ?

COLERIDGE

BECAUSE his upholsterer had presented his bill, and because the amount was more than he had any very clear prospects of being able to pay, Samuel Taylor Coleridge ran away from his undergraduate days at Cambridge, and enlisted as a dragoon under the name of Silas Tomkyn Comberbacke. He says that he got the name from a shop-front, but one suspects that he made it up: he would give up his name, but would stick to his initials. Then he could still think of himself as S. T. C., and so have some hold on his personality. He was a man with no very firm hold on anything; perhaps of all the English sons of Adam his was the weakest hold. To common men like ourselves, who know so well who we are and what we are about, if so little satisfied by the one or the other, the looseness of Coleridge's hold on his personality is barely credible. How, we ask, could he, writing to Mary Evans, with whom, he still a young man, he had persuaded himself he was in love,—how could he say to Mary, 'Really, I have written so long, that I had forgot to whom I was writing'? How could he do it? The world would have to be changed from top to bottom before one of us, writing to his Mary Evans, could for an instant forget to whom he was writing.

Coleridge had a hold, even a firm one, on the fact that he was S. T. C., and he knew amazingly of what strange ingredients S. T. C. was made up; so that he was always under a sort of divine compulsion to speak the truth about himself, however much it might be against him. He could say, to get himself out of some difficulty, that he was writing a book that in fact he was not writing, even that he had written a book that in fact he had not written; he could write in a state of emotion in which the lie made the greater part; but, if he was writing seriously about himself, he must speak with divine insight. He must say such things as 'God or Chaos preserve me! What but infinite Wisdom or infinite Confusion can do it?' Either would have done; infinite Wisdom necessarily; but infinite confusion would have done almost equally as well; for make the creation confusion, and S. T. C. would have been quite at home in it. He had it as a necessity of his nature both to have nothing definite to be, and nothing definite to do. He once advertised (Mr. Hugh I'Anson Fausset and his 'Samuel Taylor Coleridge' are my guides in this strange world, as he more than any one will recognize) that on a certain day he would lecture on *Romeo and Juliet*. He might not have turned up at all; not a few times, when he was advertised to lecture, he did not put in an appearance. This particular time he did present himself to his gathered audience.

As I have said, he was to lecture on *Romeo and Juliet*. He began with a defence of school-flogging. Why I do not know, but it may have been that something had just reminded him of Southey (he may have passed some one in the street like Southey), who, he would know, had been expelled from Westminster School by a head master without a sense of humour for contributing to *The Flagellant*, a periodical that he was editing, an article attacking corporal punishment. That might have been it, but one knows nothing for certain. S. T. C. passed from his defence of school-flogging to the characters of Queen Elizabeth and King James I as compared with the character of Charles I. He then distinguished, but not very clearly, they say, between wit and fancy; referred to the different languages of Europe; attacked the fashionable notion concerning poetic diction, and then warmly defended Shakespeare against the charge of impurity. That might have reminded him that he had come there to lecture on *Romeo and Juliet*, but it did not. That was the kind of looseness of hold that S. T. C. had on things.

Did he decide deliberately, on the way to the lecture room, some one may ask, that he would not lecture on *Romeo and Juliet*? No, no; that was not how things happened with him. Moral obligation, he once confessed, was to him so strong a stimulant, that in nine cases out of ten it acted as a narcotic. When I read that in Mr. Fausset's book, I got up and took my Commonplace Book, and immediately wrote the thing down. I do not think I had ever read anything that caught me so by the throat. To feel so strongly that you must do a thing that by and by the very strength of the feeling made you forget the thing, so that you got off without doing it—if most is to be learned from extremes, how much, I said, is not to be learned from this man? So it is: Coleridge had the most interesting mind, for the purpose of one's study, of any one on earth. With that thought fixed firmly in one's mind, it is safe to read his Life, which, without that thought, it is safe for no one to read; for it is a story of failure that makes one's impotence to do anything to help just too painful.

His greatest work was *The Rime of the Ancient Mariner*, perhaps the most successful poem that has ever been written in English; a poem that an

English sailor may know well, who knows no other poem at all. How did S. T. C. contrive to write it? The story has often been told, but it will bear telling again. I have often read it: I read it again in Mr. Fausset's book with undiminished interest. It cannot be rightly told by one who should begin the story with the day on which the first line of the poem was written. The story properly begins further back than that; indeed, a long way further back. It divides itself into two parts.

Coleridge had taken a cottage at Stowey, a village nestling at the foot of the heathy Quantocks, from whose tops in summer weather there was a view to be had of the Mendip hills to the north and beyond to the Welsh mountains faintly pencilled in blue along the sky-line. There was a kitchen garden and an orchard, and Coleridge was to raise 'potatoes and all manner of vegetables'. 'I am already an expert gardener,' he one day reported. Amusement is never far off in this story; amusement and misery here are bed-fellows. He had to admit later that the garden was covered with weeds, but that he explained as due to his equalitarian principles, since he thought it unfair to prejudice the soil 'towards roses and strawberries'. So some men have seen in their principles (reading 'principle' where we may be forgiven if we read 'egotism') a reason why they should not prejudice their children's minds in favour of God and good. If Coleridge thought it unfair to prejudice the soil of his kitchen garden in favour of strawberries, equally unfair would it have been to set a trap in the cottage to catch mice, and Sara Coleridge's life was made a pest by them. Little Hartley was too young to watch them.

Suddenly to the sum of Coleridge's life Dorothy Wordsworth was added. He had not had hold enough upon himself to do anything, unless idle reading, dreaming of pantisocracy, and the writing of insipid verse count as doing things; but if there was some one at hand who could hold him to something, then he might do all that the occasion inspired. The world will never know all that it has lost from Dorothy's not seeing clearly (but how could she be expected to see?) how much she could have made Coleridge do by giving her whole mind to holding him tight. She did hold him tight for a time, but not knowing that she was doing it. She did it simply by going for walks with Coleridge in the woods round Stowey, and talking about the things that interested herself. Hers was a life between banks. His was a sea without a shore, just a waste of water. But he had a great gift for sympathy, the sympathy that is commonly

called a 'woman's sympathy', but is far deeper than
hers, and he could flow, at least for a time, between another's banks. Then her hold on things
(it is to be noted that it was always a woman) for
the time being was his hold.

We know what Dorothy Wordsworth talked to
Coleridge about during their walks together in the
Stowey woods and on the Quantocks, because she
kept a journal, and the things that she wrote in it
reappeared in the poems that he wrote at that
time. Other men write poems about what they see
or feel in themselves. The feeling may have as its
generating subject some thing or some one outside themselves; but the feeling itself is in themselves. There was nothing definite enough either
of seeing or feeling in Coleridge himself (I ought
to say that I have read words that partly contradict
this) for any poetry to be born of it: he was too
formless or shapeless; but let him suspend himself,
and take up another's being—he could then write,
he did then write, the most haunting things in the
English language. It may be that other men's
poems are less haunting because of the measure
of egotism in them; the measure that was not in
Coleridge. If a man is to write poems about himself that shall be haunting for other men, I suppose
he must see himself as so far off, that he then is as

good as another person. A recent writer in the
Literary Supplement of *The Times* had this:
'The poet must even, as Keats was the first to
understand, objectify his own emotions before he
can make poetic use of them.' But I am not writing an essay on the psychology of poetry.

The Wordsworths, brother and sister, were
staying at Alfoxden, within walking distance of
Stowey. As Dorothy and Coleridge walked to
and fro between Stowey and Alfoxden, she would
show him the first strawberry flower under the
hedge, the locks of wool, spotted with red, that
the sheep had left upon the paling, the vapour
sliding in one mighty mass upon the sea-shore, and
how the distant country, overhung by straggling
clouds, seemed itself like a bank of darker cloud.
She would bid him listen to the snow dripping
from the holly boughs, and to the slender notes of
a redbreast. She would write in her journal: 'A
cloudy sky. Observed nothing particularly interesting—the distant prospect obscured. One only
leaf upon the top of a tree—the sole remaining
leaf—danced round and round like a rag blown by
the wind.' Or: 'A sort of white shade over the
blue sky. The stars dim. The spring continues
to advance very slowly, no green trees, the hedges
leafless, nothing green but the brambles that still

retain their old leaves. The crooked arm of the old oak tree points upwards to the moon.' Or she would write: 'The night cloudy but not dark.' That had been the matter of her talk with Coleridge. Then he would write in *Christabel*:

Is the night chilly and dark?
The night is chilly, but not dark.
The thin gray cloud is spread on high,
It covers but not hides the sky.
The moon is behind, and at the full;
And yet she looks both small and dull.
The night is chill, the cloud is gray:
'Tis a month before the month of May,
And the Spring comes slowly up this way.

She stole along, she nothing spoke,
The sighs she heaved were soft and low,
And nought was green upon the oak
But moss and rarest mistletoe.
She kneels beneath the huge oak tree,
And in silence prayeth she.

The night is chill; the forest bare;
Is it the wind that moaneth bleak?
There is not wind enough in the air
To move away the ringlet curl
From the lovely lady's cheek—
There is not wind enough to twirl
The one red leaf, the last of its clan,
That dances as often as dance it can,

Hanging so light, and hanging so high,
On the topmost twig that looks up at the sky.

It was the Coleridge so controlled who set out with Dorothy and Wordsworth on a walk that was to begin as a walk to Watchet, but was to be extended thence as far along the coast as Lynton and the Valley of the Stones. Their expenses were to be defrayed by a poem for which they hoped to get £5. A friend had recently told Coleridge of a dream in which a skeleton ship was manned by a ghostly navigator, and the dream reminded him of books of travel that he had read, and especially of one telling of a miraculous shipwreck. All this was talked of; for they had to find a subject for their poem. Wordsworth was reminded of something that he had read—how a man while doubling Cape Horn had frequently seen an albatross. 'Suppose', he said to Coleridge, 'you make the ghostly navigator have killed an albatross.'

The idea fired Coleridge. He forthwith spoke the first lines of *The Rime*, as one repeating an incantation:

It is an ancient Mariner,
And he stoppeth one of three.
'By thy long grey beard and glittering eye,
Now wherefore stopp'st thou me?

'The Bridegroom's doors are open'd wide,
And I am next of kin;
The guests are met, the feast is set—
May'st hear the merry din.'

He holds him with his skinny hand.
'There was a ship,' quoth he.
'Hold off! unhand me, grey-beard loon!'
Eftsoons his hand dropt he.

He holds him with his glittering eye . . .

Wordsworth gave that last line, but if you will look you will see that it is made all of words that Coleridge has already used; so it really should count as Coleridge's own. Wordsworth contributed some other lines, the best of them, and they are very good lines indeed, being:

And thou art long, and lank, and brown
As is the ribbed sea-sand.

He contributed those lines and a few more, but had afterwards to leave it all to the other; for Coleridge by that time was in a world in which no Wordsworth ever breathed:

The very deep did rot: O Christ!
That ever this should be!
Yea, slimy things did crawl with legs
Upon the slimy sea.

About, about, in reel and rout,
The death-fires danced at night;

The water, like a witch's oils,
Burnt green, and blue, and white . . .

Ah! well a-day! what evil looks
Had I from old and young!
Instead of the cross, the albatross
About my neck was hung.

That was a world in which Wordsworth could not breathe. It was as little one in which Dorothy could. If Coleridge had not been Coleridge, that is, a man the doors of whose subconscious mind could open in waking life as well as in the dream-life, then Dorothy could not have written *The Rime* and *Christabel*, as far as she may be said to have written them. Now to believe that such a man, even such a man controlled, could write the greatest poetry in his language—that is more than it is reasonable to ask any one to believe. If *The Ancient Mariner* and *Christabel* are the most haunting of poems to Englishmen generally, it is a proof how little growth in emotion the English race has made; a proof that the race is still a childish thing. There is English poetry compared with which these two poems of Coleridge's, with *Kubla Khan* added, are—just nothing. That is the conclusion to which one must come, however one may stray by the way. I feel in myself a separation between the emotional child to which verse that is

more incantation than thought appeals and an
older being emotionally, the being to which the
poetry appeals that is a much deeper revelation of
God. It would be easy to deny and starve the latter
being; to let oneself be carried so far by the lure of
incantation, that the great Mount of God would
rise no longer above the horizon; but that is for-
bidden. The call upon one is to have courage, and
go out into all the Wildernesses of Temptation that
there are. When they have been passed through,
one's chosen reading will far oftener be such as:

all Oracles

By thee are giv'n, and what confest more true
Among the Nations? that hath been thy craft,
By mixing somewhat true to vent more lyes.
But what have been thy answers, what but dark
Ambiguous and with double sense deluding,
Which they who ask'd have seldom understood,
And not well understood as good not known?
Who ever by consulting at thy shrine
Return'd the wiser, or the more instruct
To flye or follow what concern'd him most,
And run not sooner to his fatal snare?
For God hath justly giv'n the Nations up
To thy Delusions; justly, since they fell
Idolatrous, but when his purpose is
Among them to declare His Providence
To thee not known, whence hast thou then thy truth,

But from him or his Angels President
In every Province, who themselves disdaining
To approach thy Temples, give thee in command
What to the smallest tittle thou shalt say
To thy Adorers; thou with trembling fear,
Or like a Fawning Parasite obey'st;
Then to thy self ascrib'st the truth foretold.
But this thy glory shall be soon retrench'd;
No more shalt thou by oracling abuse
The Gentiles; henceforth Oracles are ceast,
And thou no more with Pomp and Sacrifice
Shalt be enquired at *Delphos* or elsewhere,
At least in vain, for they shall find thee mute.
God hath now sent his living Oracle
Into the World, to teach his final will,
And sends his Spirit of truth henceforth to dwell
In pious hearts, an inward Oracle
To all truth requisite to men to know.

Read that again, read it three times, and then
read what I have quoted from *Christabel*, and you
must see that Milton is writing men's poetry and
Coleridge children's only. It is because we are
such children that we are so ready for *The Elegy*,
The Rime, Childe Harold, The Shropshire Lad, and
so not ready for Milton and Dante. I said so
once to Mrs. Rosenthal, a contemporary writer
on poetry, and she broke in, exclaiming: 'I know,
I know—picture-book poetry!'

POETRY AND EXPERIENCE

THERE are subjects, and religion and poetry are two of them, that are of such absorbing interest, that men will go on thinking and writing about them as long as there are men to think and write. It is of poetry that I have thought most; asking myself questions, and answering them, but it might not be until after the thought of years. Among those questions have been, first, the eternal question, 'What is poetry?' and then these others, 'How are we to tell great poetry from lesser poetry?' and, 'Is the poetry of any day, and consequently the poetry of our own day, to be judged exactly as all other poetry, or may the nature of poetry so change, that the judging has to be by new and other rules?'

Matthew Arnold tried to answer the question, 'What is poetry?' Poetry, he said, is a criticism of life; and he tried to teach us how to tell great poetry from lesser poetry. We were to have certain touchstones, and we were to judge any poem by applying those touchstones. It may be doubted if to say that poetry is a criticism of life is not too likely merely to suggest the question,

'What is criticism of life ?' In other words, the objection to the definition is that it does not say anything clear enough. As to the touchstones, it may be doubted if any one who could judge a poem by applying them, could not judge it as well without (it might be by unconsciously applying them), or if, in fact, any considerable number of persons have learned to apply touchstones, or are likely ever to do so. That is not to say that Arnold's essay is not a profoundly pregnant piece of writing, but merely that it is only that for the few.

It might be helpful to defer the attempt to answer the question, 'What is poetry?' until we have answered the easier question, 'What is not poetry?' It is clear that the thing called 'poem' has undergone many changes since the first one was written; that many things that are called poems are poems only in some other sense of the word. There is seen, at the first glance, to be a world of difference between the Vedic Hymns, the *Iliad*, and the Book of Job and such things as *The Rape of the Lock*, *Bishop Blougram's Apology*, and Locker-Lampson's *London Lyrics*. Charles Lamb would have written *The Rape of the Lock* as an essay; a different Browning would have written *Bishop Blougram's Apology* as a prose dialogue, and the *London Lyrics* might have been written as letters. These, then, in one sense at least, are seen not to be poetry, and with them whole libraries in verse are seen not to be poetry. There may be a clue in this to what poetry is.

If these writings are only prose thought in metrical form, is it not probable that poetry is something rarer, more difficult, secret? If it is a secret, what is it the secret of? It is the secret, I should say, of anything of perennial interest; but it is that secret wrested with difficulty (except that genius, which alone can write poetry, does whatever it does easily). If a man without genius could be thought of as wresting the secret (we know he could not do it), he could wrest it, we feel sure, with great labour and difficulty. Nothing that could be got at by sheer dint of intelligent thinking, or observation of natural things, will be poetry in the highest sense of the word. If, to make the matter clearer, I go on to quote pieces of verse in which the secrets of things are revealed, the apparent ease with which the poets are seen to have reached them must not mislead us. What must be borne in mind is the difficulty, rather the impossibility, of their being reached by any merely intelligent thinking.

I have said nothing that Arnold has not already said in a page of his essay on Maurice de Guérin, a page of such value, be it said in passing, that anything wrong in Arnold's having written about such a one as de Guérin should be forgiven for its sake. 'It is not Linnaeus,' Arnold writes, 'or Cavendish, or Cuvier who gives us the true sense of animals, or water, or plants, who seizes their secret for us, who makes us participate in their life; it is Shakespeare, with his

> daffodils
> That come before the swallow dares, and take
> The winds of March with beauty;

it is Wordsworth, with his

> voice . . . heard
> In spring-time from the cuckoo-bird,
> Breaking the silence of the seas
> Among the farthest Hebrides;

it is Keats, with his

> Moving waters at their priestlike task
> Of pure ablution round earth's human shores.'

What makes all those passages belong to the greatest poetry is that a secret hidden from the common man is revealed in each. There are no secrets revealed in the two passages, the first from Tennyson, the second from Byron, that follow, and that is what makes them not great poetry. There is nothing in them, not a single word, that could

not be reached merely by intelligent thinking, or
by observation.

> Elaine the fair, Elaine the lovable,
> Elaine, the lily maid of Astolat,
> High in her chamber up a tower to the east
> Guarded the sacred shield of Lancelot;
> Which first she placed where morning's earliest ray
> Might strike it, and awake her with the gleam;
> Then fearing rust or soilure fashion'd for it
> A case of silk, and braided thereupon
> All the devices blazon'd on the shield
> In their own tinct, and added, of her wit,
> A border fantasy of branch and flower,
> And yellow-throated nestling in the nest.

> They looked up to the sky, whose floating glow
> Spread like a rosy ocean, vast and bright;
> They gazed upon the glittering sea below
> Whence the broad moon rose circling into sight—
> They heard the waves plash, and the wind so low,
> And saw each other's dark eyes darting light
> Into each other; and beholding this
> Their lips grew near and clung into a kiss.

Shakespeare wrote the quoted words, as Wordsworth his, and Keats his, in a moment of sudden
inspiration, an illumination, which then went out,
bringing common day again. Byron was not inspired; he saw what he was writing about with his
human eyes only: Tennyson was not illuminated;

that was part of the morning's exercise for a man
for whom poetry was mostly the sound of words,
a man writing for people, childish people, for
whom poetry was the sound of words. Neither
Byron nor Tennyson had the sense of the poet as
a diviner being than other men, waiting for the
breath of inspiration, the breath that had come
before, but could not be called, and might never
come again; a man, so, living in awe. Neither
Byron nor Tennyson was such a man as Blake, one
who knew that, if he dwelt apart in spirit, and
brooded long enough, God might speak to him;
that out of the very dust of the earth the suddenly
flashed flower might spring.

To go back to Arnold's examples of the greatest
poetry. Where, in each one, a secret is revealed,
or to use Arnold's word, the true sense is given, as
science could not give it, the thing is done by the
essence of one thing being shown in the light of
another thing; and it is certain, to my mind, that
it can be done as poetry in no other way. It is the
bringing together in our minds of the daffodil and
the swallow's coming that makes clear to us that
our thought of the daffodil is not what it would be,
if the daffodil had its flowers in autumn. It is the
thought of beauty softening something harsh, as
the beauty of a child, or a woman, or music might

soften something harsh in a man, that brings out
so much more of what the daffodil is. It is seen as
more beautiful for coming in spring; for coming
when our hearts are empty of beauty because of
the winter sleep. Then there is seen to be something of courage suggested by the shape, poise,
and colour of the daffodil—there is, that is to say,
after Shakespeare has opened our eyes to it. That
courage, which it is enough for us that the poet
should just hint at, is shown in the light of the
swallow's daring. It is only in inspired poetry
that so much can be given in so few words; so that
one's definition of poetry might be that it is the
inspired word. There is nothing that a poet may
not forget, so long as he remembers that his word
must be inspired.

It is only, to pass on, if we also think of the
silence, not so real as easily imagined, for there is
the continual noise of the wind and waters, of the
seas among the farthest Hebrides, that the secret
of the appeal for us in the cuckoo's voice is revealed. So of Keats's lines: it is the bringing together in our minds of the thought of water,
priesthood, and ablution, that reveals the secret
of the seas round the shores of the earth; of the
pureness of water compared with the impurity of
human life. The thing is seen more clearly, when

Shakespeare does it again and again in one crowded passage, as in:

> She should have died hereafter;
> There would have been a time for such a word.
> To-morrow, and to-morrow, and to-morrow,
> Creeps in this petty pace from day to day,
> To the last syllable of recorded time;
> And all our yesterdays have lighted fools
> The way to dusty death. Out, out, brief candle!
> Life's but a walking shadow, a poor player
> That struts and frets his hour upon the stage,
> And then is heard no more; it is a tale
> Told by an idiot, full of sound and fury,
> Signifying nothing.

There must be something deep in the constitution of the human mind to account for this, that nothing can be thoroughly known, in such a way as will satisfy the psyche's deepest craving to know, unless it is shown in the light of the nature of some other thing. It may be that all things are ultimately one, and that what we crave for, and what poetry more than anything else helps us to, is the vision of them all as one.

There must, then, be a revelation of the secrets of things. Words are things, and they have their secrets too. I will not beg any question by speaking of the beauty of words, but will be content to speak simply of their secret. It is revealed wonder-

fully in the following verse, but, I think, no other
secret is, which is what makes it not great
poetry:

> What thing unto mine ear
> Wouldst thou convey,—what secret thing,
> O wandering water ever whispering?
> Surely thy speech shall be of her,
> Thou water, O thou whispering wanderer,
> What message dost thou bring?

So, too, in:

> Le temps s'en va, le temps s'en va, ma dame;
> Las, le temps non, mais nous nous en allons,

it is doubtful to me if anything is revealed but the
secret of words. No, it is not doubtful; I see that
nothing else is; nothing, that is, to prove those
words inspired.

I assume, then, that the greatest poetry must
reveal the secret of things, and the secrets of words
at the same time. Can that not be done in prose?
Undoubtedly it can be, and one may be prepared
to go with any one who prefers to write his poetry
as prose, as one is prepared to go with Milton in
preferring blank verse to rhyme for its greater
freedom. The addition of metre in the work of
one whom it does not hamper, but helps, will
clearly, however, be so much more. The greatest
art must have a rhythm that is an echo of the

rhythm of melody by which we think of the stars as kept in their courses.

If the nature of great poetry be such as I imagine it, it is clear that it can never change; so neither could the rules by which it is to be judged. If our concern is with a poem of our own day, it must be judged to be the greatest poetry, however the outward fashion of it may be different from the older poetry, only if it reveals the secrets of deep, perennial things, and the secret of words too. If it only reveals the secret of the passing emotion aroused by the departure of the Scotch express from Euston, and by the steam left behind in the railway station, nothing should persuade us that it is the greatest poetry, or even great poetry, or even in the deepest sense poetry at all. One may write, and very interestingly too, in verse, of all sorts of things; but poetry must be written by an awed man, by one with the sense of being dedicated. And he must not deceive himself.

There is an apparent contradiction, as I may admit before passing on, in dismissing *The Rape of the Lock* and the others as not great poetry simply because they could be written as prose, and then in admitting that great poetry could be written in prose. My thought was that they, written as prose, would be, to put it familiarly, of prose prosy, which the Book of Job never could be, though the *Iliad* perhaps could.

I would put it forward, not as a scientific thing or to be read too literally, that the explanation of the fact of there having been so few men able to write the greatest poetry, which is to reveal the secret of things by showing them in the light of other things, and to reveal the secret of words at the same time (perhaps of melody also)—I put it forward that the explanation of that is, and that the explanation of the relatively small quantity of the greatest poetry in the writings of the great poets is, that the faculty requisite for such poetry is such as the unconscious-mind imagination; a thing, that is, of which man has not the use at will, as he has the use of his intellect. It may be taken as certain that the greatest poetry will never be written except by a man, moving indeed among men, but with the mind of a recluse; it will be the result of a continual brooding over things. And the quantity of it will always be small. It may be a larger quantity in future for men's seeing better what it is.

The greatest poetry I credit, then, to the unconscious-mind imagination. Is there no part left for the conscious mind? Undoubtedly there is a part. It can give us, not the secret of things

shown in the light of some other things, but anything as the thoughtful mind has seen it; not
something divine, a thing that the man was inspired to say, but what that man's mind has seen,
and pondered over, and understood. If at the same
time there is a revelation of the secret of words and
rhythm, then we shall have what is great poetry,
but not the greatest; what is of great human
interest, if without the power to thrill and en-
rapture. I call such poetry to myself, for to have
names for classes is an aid to thought, *rhetoric*.

> *Fame* is the spur that the clear spirit doth raise
> (That last infirmity of Noble mind)
> To scorn delights, and live laborious dayes;
> But the fair Guerdon when we hope to find,
> And think to burst out into sudden blaze,
> Comes the blind *Fury* with th'abhorred shears,
> And slits the thin spun life,—

is for me the class of the greatest poetry, because
I cannot conceive of any conscious mind simply
thinking that out; but

> Had we never loved so kindly,
> Had we never loved so blindly,
> Never met and never parted,
> We had ne'er been broken-hearted,

and

> For we are born in others' pain,
> And perish in our own

are not the greatest poetry, but what I call rhetoric;
for I can conceive a conscious mind simply thinking them out. For

> The sun to me is dark,
> And silent as the moon,
> When she deserts the night,
> Hid in her vacant interlunar cave,—

for that, for it to be credible to me that men should
be able to write things like that (apart from my
seeing them), it is necessary that I should believe
that there is something known to exist by which
a man can be inspired. That something known to
exist, or, if not known, then, in the words of
Collins, dim-discovered, is the unconscious-mind
imagination.

> The fleecy star that bears
> Andromeda far off Atlantic seas . . .

> Not that faire field
> Of Enna, where Proserpin gathring flours
> Her self a fairer Floure by gloomie Dis
> Was gatherd, which cost Ceres all that pain
> To seek her through the world—

those may be a little more than rhetoric, but I
think they are not; and certainly the following are
clearly not: they are just rhetoric:

We men, who in our morn of youth defied
The elements, must vanish;—be it so!

Enough, if something from our hands have power
To live, and act, and serve the future hour;
And if, as toward the silent tomb we go,
Through love, through hope, and faith's transcendent
      power,
We feel that we are greater than we know;

and

> To me the meanest flower that blows can give
> Thoughts that do often lie too deep for tears.

Those are just rhetoric.

For the writing of the greatest poetry there must
be that passing up of things from the unconscious
mind-imagination into the conscious mind without which the fruit would remain unharvested,
and we can only think of these men as born with
the doors between the two as able to open. The
power of revealing the secret of words will be
inborn too. For rhetoric there must be, then, so
much of the inborn. What else? What there must
be for any wise thinking—an adequate experience
of life. Something must be said about experience
of life.

Shakespeare's plays and *The Divine Comedy* are
not the greatest poetry throughout, but what is
not the greatest poetry is most of it what I have
called rhetoric. Page after page of Wordsworth,
of Swinburne in his plays, and of Tennyson in his

plays and many of his poems, are neither the greatest poetry, nor rhetoric, but just nothing to any purpose. Not all of that, to my mind, is to be ascribed to difference in the poetic calibre of the men, but to this—that, however inadequate may have been the experience of life of Shakespeare and Dante for the purpose of poetry (to my mind it was nothing inadequate, but another might think differently), it was not as the experience of Wordsworth, Swinburne, and Tennyson, which, as a whole, was utterly inadequate. The burden of all FitzGerald's criticism of the later Tennyson, and very sound criticism I consider it, is that the man, never having been in close contact with the affairs of men, and now living in seclusion, guarded by his wife from even such contact with the rough world as is involved in a man's answering his friends' letters, had no experience out of which to go on making poetry. FitzGerald will write:

'I have just finished the fourth Book of Thucydides . . . This fourth book is the most interesting I have read . . . and it came upon me "come stella in ciel" when, in the account of the taking of Amphipolis, Thucydides . . . comes with seven ships to the rescue. Fancy Old Hallam sticking to his gun at a Martello tower. That was the way to write well; and this was the way to make literature respectable. Oh, Alfred Tennyson, could you but have the luck to be put to such employment.'

And again:

'It is the cursed inactivity (very pleasant to me who am no Hero) of this nineteenth century which has spoiled Alfred, I mean spoiled him for the great work he ought now to be entering upon; the lovely and noble things he has done must remain.'

And again:

'I have long felt about England as you do. . . . If one could save the Race, what a Cause it would be! not for one's own glory as a member of it, nor even for its glory as a Nation; but because it is the only spot in Europe where Freedom keeps her place. Had I Alfred's voice, I would not have mumbled for years over In Memoriam and the Princess, but sung such strains as would have revived the Μαραθωνομάχους ἄνδρας to guard the territory they had won. But what can "In Memoriam" do but make us all sentimental?'

It will be understood that a poet's experience of life may have been utterly inadequate to make three-fourths of his book poetry, while quite adequate to make the remainder poetry. (I am not at the moment concerned with the distinction between the greatest poetry and rhetoric.) You would have in mere dark misery and hunger in the streets experience adequate to the writing of:

> For we are born in others' pain,
> And perish in our own.

It will also be understood that what was the

sum of his experience to a man, the circumstances
of his life having been such or such, would not
have been exactly the sum of that experience to
another man. To Carlyle the railway journey to
Scotland would always have been a greater experience than to, say, Coventry Patmore. The reading
of a book was nine times out of ten a greater
experience to Browning than reading the same
book was to Tennyson.

What should be understood is that the technical
gift, power of mouthing melodies, is alone not
enough; that if a man knows little or nothing of
life, never having had any contact with it to speak
of, his 'great' play will be a great dreariness and
weariness, and had better not be written. There
must be the dwelling in the seclusion of the mind,
the continual brooding over things, for otherwise,
without that, the door of the unconscious-mind
imagination never opens: what Arnold wrote is
true:

> hurt to death she lay!
> Shuddering, they drew her garments off—and found
> A robe of sackcloth next the smooth, white skin.
> Such, poets, is your bride, the Muse! young, gay,
> Radiant, adorned outside; a hidden ground
> Of thought and of austerity within,

but life, wherever it can be got hold of, must be

laid hold of with both hands. How Shakespeare must have done that, how he mixed eagerly with men, yet with a mind continually withdrawn, is very well set forth in Lafcadio Hearn's lecture on him.

One passes easily from the thought that a poet must have had an adequate experience of life (it is most crowded, that experience, in the councils where men's affairs are considered) to the thought that he should write of the life that he has experienced, using the language that he and his contemporaries talk. Matthew Arnold's advice that he should use some old Greek, Hebrew, or Norse subject (for the benefit of having a subject that men are already familiar with. Are we already familiar with the subject of *Balder Dead*? I should not be, even after five readings, ten years after the fifth), and the example of Tennyson and others, making plays of the story of Mary Tudor and the like, and writing them in the language of:

In this low pulse and palsy of the state,—

that seems to me very poor advice to give, and a very wrong example to follow. It is not a matter that very well lends itself to argument: if a man does not see it for himself, what can be said? See it, I mean of course, not while Arnold's advice is being read, but while *Balder Dead* is, or your

historical play by Tennyson. One can write a live
historical play as Shakespeare did, filling the stage,
God forgiving the anachronism, with the men and
women who walk up and down Fleet Street in
one's own day, and making Caesar or King Lear
or Desdemona talk as they would talk, were they
English men and women of the author's day. Try
to recapture the very thought of men of five cen-
turies ago, and express it in their language, and
your poem or play is dead before it is born.
Browning had the sense to make Karshish talk
exactly like Robert Browning.

Part of the experience that a man must have, if
his experience of life is to be the fullest, is, it is
arguable, the experience of being read or acted.
That part must nowadays be given him; he cannot
take it for himself, which is the more the pity,
since fewer and fewer people now read poetry;
since fewer and fewer can read it, the most failing
to get even the bare grammatical sense. But if
a man can take that experience, let him: let him do
anything that he can to force the world of his own
day to read him. It is no use dying, as a critic in
the Literary Supplement to *The Times* once said
that Flecker died—'of loneliness, exile, and
neglect'—and it is no use hoping that the fact of
Flecker having so died will help *you*. That critic is

not trying to prevent anybody else from dying in the same way, nor is anybody else.

If the professional critics were bigger men, and not so given to 'coterie-praise' of their own choice, if they worked for editors who were bigger men, not so given, for their choice, to requiring 'sheep-praise' of their reviewers, with the result that all the reviews of any week or month are always almost all about the same books, and for the most part always about the same old writers, the experience of being read would come to most writers sooner. There are, I know, two or three fine, even great, critics working to-day for the periodical press, and they use an independent judgement; but the fact was in the past that the important writings were not read until late; and there is nothing in the general appearance of the way in which criticism is gone about at this day to make one suppose that any more prompt attention is bestowed now.

The literary judgements of each generation are all modified subsequently, and many of them are completely upset. This would be less often so, perhaps, if a certain saying had not become current, or, having become current, had been more deeply considered. The saying is that every great poet must create the taste by which he is to be appre-

ciated. The objection to the saying is that it does
not say anything clear enough, and, in particular,
that it leaves us to discover for ourselves how the
thing is done. How does the great poet create the
taste, or rather, for of course he does not do it, by
whom is the taste created, and how is it done?
Those are the pregnant questions.

I think it is certain that, if there is a general,
worthy appreciation of the old poets, which surely
there is, an appreciation of which we may be proud
and not ashamed, it is because people have taken
the requisite trouble; both those whose business it
is to write about the old poets, and those who make
it their pleasure to read them. I need not concern
myself with more than the readers. If many of us
now living have a worthy appreciation of Shakespeare, Milton, Vaughan, Wordsworth, Shelley,
Keats, Blake, what is the explanation? Their
contemporaries had not. It is not that we are so
very able, that we are such good judges naturally,
but that their works were passed to us by men
speaking with the authority of time; men who
said in effect: 'If you do not appreciate all these
worthily, it will be a thing for shame;' and it was
their saying that that made us take the requisite
trouble. Taking the requisite trouble meant reading each poem often enough; often enough, both

for the appreciation of that poem, and for the acquisition of some measure of a general power to appreciate poetry. It was we who created this generation's taste for each poet, doing it within ourselves. We did it by reading poems often enough. Let a man to-day read *Lycidas*, and then let him try to measure his enjoyment of the poem to-day and his enjoyment of it the first, or even the fifth, time of his reading it. He cannot do it. The power grew in him so slowly, that there was never any measuring it.

What is wrong with the criticism of the writings of the critics' contemporaries is always that it is written by men who have not read their authors carefully enough, and that it is written for people who will not do that either, if I may count their reading as part of the criticism. In a perfectly organized republic of letters one critic would be told off for each writer, so that there might be one living critic who knew his man as well as we know our Keats. Each great poet and each fine poem would then be recognized so much the sooner; and that would be a good thing; for though, there being already so many great poets for the delight of the world, one more or less can make little difference, yet not to recognize a poet until he is old or dead is an unkindness to him, and an unkindness for which we or others after us will pay; for if a poet is neglected who should not be neglected, his experience of life is so much the poorer, and his poetry so much the poorer in consequence. It is made poorer, or, which is worse, it is made wrong.

THE GREATEST POETRY

A CRITIC, writing of Professor Abercrombie's *The Idea of Great Poetry*, says:

Mr. Abercrombie is concerned to insist that, in poetry as in the other arts, the supreme greatness demands scale. Nothing that he has to say is more opportune than this. Our generation, in its lack of leisure and its worship of detail, tends to forget that a cottage may indeed be as architecturally perfect as a cathedral, a song as musically perfect as a symphony, an epitaph as poetically perfect as an epic; but that, if all are equally perfect, it necessarily follows that the epic, the symphony, and the cathedral are greater than the epitaph, song, and cottage. Their perfection involves a far wider range of experience, demands a far richer expression of mind and emotion and imagination. To take the old illustration, the pint pot and the quart measure may be equally full, but that does not make them equal. What is a poem? It is an experience of one person expressed in such language, at once exact and enchanting, that it becomes the experience of another, of many others. Four lines of Sappho or Simonides may effect that transition with the completeness of absolute felicity. But the experience so transmitted cannot have scale or variety; it cannot contain, as the *Iliad* contains, the whole complex wonder of life.

That is a good text. In dealing with it I shall repeat a little of what I have written elsewhere.

In a matter in which opinions are so much in conflict, a little repetition may be allowed.

To begin with a small matter. By dint of repeating that this generation lacks leisure, people have induced themselves to believe that it does. The falseness of it might be held to be proved by its being repeated with so little real regret; by no man's pausing to consider how the lost leisure —leisure being the greatest good in life, if wisely used—could be recovered. If we slept more hours, took longer to procure our food, or to eat it, or, which is perhaps to say the same thing and more, had to work longer hours, then we should have less leisure than the men of the past; but we do not and have not to. We have, in the far greater knowledge of the working of the human body, in the greater knowledge of how to rest, the power to make less sleep and less food do us as much good as the sleep we still take and the food we eat. That would be the road to gaining still more leisure. We have as much as men ever have had. If many fritter away so much more of it than their fathers did, it is their choice.

The only wise thing to say is that we have as much leisure, or, if we have not, that it is a disgrace. It is wrong to go on complacently saying that we have less.

The greatest poetry is not, I should say, the experience of one person expressed in such language that it becomes the experience of others. The greatest poetry is of the nature of a revelation—to one man, and is by him communicated to others. In a sense it is or becomes as little the writer's experience as it becomes the experience of others. I am now speaking, of course, of the experience of the hour of writing the poem, of the flowering time of that expression. There may be an earlier experience, the experience of something lived, out of which that experience of self-expression in song grew. The writer has the latter experience—of its vivifying soul for some instants, and revivifying his soul whenever he reads the words with his being at sufficient intensity. For others there is only the parallel to the latter experience. The revelation must be waited for as the descent of the gift of prophecy was waited for. It will come of an intensely disciplined physical life; of the keeping of the soul free of the cares that darken and burden; of the cleansing of the soul of all tendency to the corrosion wrought by anger, hate, spite, vindictiveness; of the being born again a little child such as those that make the kingdom of heaven. If any man would write the greatest poetry, such must his life be.

It is with the descent from the greatest poetry to
what is not the greatest, but is still immeasurably
great, that the material is more strictly speaking
human experience, as all men understand experience, and have felt it; and then, it is true, the
question of scale becomes important. Such a
poem, perfect in its kind, as:

> Happy were he could finish forth his fate
> In some unhaunted desert, where, obscure
> From all society, from love and hate
> Of worldly folk, there could he sleep secure;
>
> Then wake again, and yield God ever praise;
> Content with hips, with haws, and brambleberry;
> In contemplation passing still his days,
> And change of holy thoughts to make him merry:
>
> Who, when he dies, his tomb might be the bush
> Where harmless robin resteth with the thrush:
>   Happy were he!

cannot be the equal of:

>   for now too nigh
> Th' Archangel stood, and from the other Hill
> To thir fixt Station, all in bright array
> The Cherubim descended; on the ground
> Gliding meteorous, as Ev'ning Mist
> Ris'n from a River o're the marish glides,
> And gathers ground fast at the Labourers heel
> Homeward returning.   High in Front advanc't,
> The brandisht Sword of God before them blaz'd

Fierce as a Comet; which with torrid heat,
And vapour as the *Libyan* Air adust,
Began to parch that temperate Clime; whereat
In either hand the hastning Angel caught
Our lingring Parents, and to th' Eastern Gate
Led them direct, and down the Cliff as fast
To the subjected Plaine; then disappear'd.
They looking back, all th' Eastern side beheld
Of Paradise, so late thir happie seat,
Wav'd over by that flaming Brand, the Gate
With dreadful Faces throng'd and fierie Armes:
Som natural tears they drop'd, but wip'd them soon.
The World was all before them, where to choose
Thir place of rest, and Providence thir guide:
They hand in hand with wandring steps and slow,
Through Eden took thir solitarie way.

It cannot be the equal of that, partly because that is a higher theme (that might be conceivably, however, have been the subject of a short poem), but more because it is the outcome of the poet's long concentration upon that theme. Scale there, then, is seen to operate.

Neither the Earl of Essex's poem nor the passage from *Paradise Lost* is at all of the nature of a revelation or a prophecy. Each is the outcome of the dwelling of a powerful mind, and a rich one, the first upon the common error of ambition, the second upon one of the world's great stories.

All this, however, is not to say that a short poem could not come much nearer to the poetic greatness of Milton's passage than the poem of the Earl of Essex does. In fact, it is not proved, and cannot be, that a short poem could not come as near; and I for one should not care to contradict the man who should say that one short poem does come as near, namely:

I saw Eternity the other night,
Like a great ring of pure and endless light,
   All calm, as it was bright:—
And round beneath it, Time, in hours, days, years,
   Driven by the spheres,
Like a vast shadow moved; in which the World
   And all her train were hurl'd.

That would have been no better—for the long concentration of the poet's mind, that is—had it occurred in the middle of the long poem. I should say rather that Vaughan would have made no more of his subject in those different circumstances.

Side by side with the habit, for so it is, of the present-day poet's choosing a light or relatively light theme, one discerns a feeling (far too seldom yielded to, however) for great and even the greatest themes as the subjects of short poems, and that apart from sonnet-writing; for at all times

poets have lived close to the great theme, if also
to the light one, as sonnet-writers.

The long poem has for an advantage afforded
by the scale of it only one thing to my mind over
the short; namely, the quality of architectonic.
The architectonic of no short poem could conceivably equal that of the *Odyssey*; but then that
is not equalled, or even, I think, approached, by
that of any other long poem; not by that of the
Divina Commedia or *Samson Agonistes*. The *Odyssey* is a story divinely told. But architectonic is in
a way the least of all things in poetry, there being
in it least of all any power of revelation; or, if
there is some secret of the universe revealed
simply in it, who has ears for it? There is more
for man, at this early stage of the life of his mind,
to hear in

> Bring me my bow of burning gold:
> Bring me my arrows of desire,

than in any architectonic considered simply in itself.

It might be argued that the long poem has
another advantage; namely, that it affords scope
for a cumulative effect. That will depend on how
the long poem is read: the reader's part is much
the greater here. Some one once read Spenser
during a voyage in a sailing ship crossing the
Atlantic; read it with concentration, being the

only passenger, until the life of the ship, and the sound of the waves, and the mists, and the beginnings and the ending of the days, and the poem faded and melted into each other. No doubt that is how any book should be read, especially the books that deserve it most. That is, however, how few books can be read, even by a man with as much leisure as I have. To me all long poems are apt to be less long poems than many short poems, with a connecting thread running through them; and the quality of those poems varies so; some are so greatly inferior to others, that the total impression is apt to be that of many fine poems somewhat spoiled in their effect by being mingled with so many much less fine; just as the effect of the better poems in the *Golden Treasury* is spoiled by their being mingled with so much that is inferior. The poets of the past, my constantly recurring thought is, were too much given to writing at length. Their public too much demanded quantity. The public does demand quantity: how often are present-day poets reproached with the slimness of their volumes?

For the long poem—this is what I am most concerned to say—for the poem, the material of which is much more human experience than anything of the nature of sudden, transfiguring

revelation, the experience of the present-day poet
is made far too narrow. That is the best reason of
all why such poems should not be attempted now.
It is because Professor Abercrombie's book is
calculated to incite our poets to write long poems,
that I speak against it. A rich and deep enough
experience for an *Iliad*, an *Aeneid*, a *Divina Commedia*, a *Paradise Regained*, a *Samson Agonistes*, is
not possessed, and cannot be, by any man who has
not played some leading part in the management
of the highest affairs of men, or has not passed
through some long agony of thought. The experience that a schoolmaster, a doctor, a lawyer,
a merchant gathers will not suffice for more than
an *Excursion* or a *Prelude* or *The Ring and the Book*,
or an *Idyll of the King*. The experience of poets
seems to grow narrower and narrower—except as
readers. (A great deal of poetry can come from
a man's reading.) The theme of the *Divina Commedia*, as of both *Paradise Lost* and *Paradise
Regained*, is the eternal hatefulness of sin: the
vision of the poems is the vision of a sinless world.
I cannot think of any present-day poet feeling
himself sufficiently prepared by experience to take
that as his theme. I expect the theme, whenever I
open a new volume of verse, to be something comparatively slight—bare field and walls and snow,

gardens, dream-fancies, woods and birds and little
beasts; and the general impression derived from all
my reading of late verse is that hardly a poet amongst
them has anything to say of deep significance.
Their thought is of the less significant things.

There is, however, as I have already said, a
feeling-out, if far too seldom followed, for the
great theme as the subject of the short poem; and
the same life-discipline, open to any one, that is the
preparation for poems of revelation, as distinguished from poems of long and deep experience
among men, will be the preparation for the writing
of short poems having great themes for their
subject. Let men live poetry, and there will come
from their very lives that effect on their writing
that is seen in those concluding lines of *Paradise
Lost* that I have quoted; the same kind of greatness of thought and expression that is induced by
length of concentration upon a theme. After all,
unless it came from that incalculable thing, pure
genius, from what but the habitual purity and
sweep of Milton's thought came the lines that
follow; lines, be it observed, that occur in a comparatively short poem, lines to my mind not sur-
passed by anything else in Milton:

> Last came, and last did go,
> The pilot of the *Galilean* lake,

Two massy Keyes he bore of metals twain,
(The Golden opes, the Iron shuts amain)
He shook his Miter'd locks, and stern bespake,
How well could I have spared for thee, young swain,
Anow of such as for their bellies sake
Creep and intrude, and climb into the fold?
Of other care they little reck'ning make,
Than how to scramble at the shearers feast,
And shove away the worthy bidden guest.
Blind mouthes! that scarce themselves know how to hold
A sheep-hook, or have learn'd ought els the least
That to the faithfull Herdmans art belongs!
What recks it them? What need they? They are sped;
And when they list, their lean and flashy songs
Grate on their scrannel Pipes of wretched straw,
The hungry Sheep look up, and are not fed,
But swoln with wind, and the rank mist they draw,
Rot inwardly and foul contagion spread.

   In the same poem occurs:
It was that fatall and perfidious Bark
Built in th'eclipse, and rigg'd with curses dark.
That sunk so low that sacred head of thine:

which illuminates like black lightning, which
nothing could make greater; no greater gift, no
more uplift of soul, no more life-discipline; and so
still less anything gained merely from the march
and sweep of a long poem.

   Then there are such poems, having great

themes, as Wordworth's greatest,—the Ode, the Tintern Abbey lines, the finest of his sonnets; all making a body of poetry with which no single long poem of his, nor all his long poems together, can compare.

Finally there is the *Golden Treasury*, which, if revised in the light of all the study of English poetry of the years since its publication, the disfiguring poems, not a few, removed, those few equal to the best that were overlooked, and the best that have been written since, added—there would then be *the* Book of English poetry; one might almost say, the English *poem*, greater than any one single great long poem conceivable, that could be written in the language. Yet a book of all short poems.

To add equally great short poems, a few, to the Book is that to which the poet of to-day should bend all his effort.

THE FUTURE OF ENGLISH POETRY

IT is very strange that men should think of poetry, which one sees, however, that they may do, as if it was something calculable as the produce of a field is. A field may be better or worse cultivated, and yield so many quarters of corn to the acre, or so many less; but as long as it is a field, and some knowledge remains of cultivation, and there is light and moisture, an annual crop may be expected.

Men will write of the future of poetry, predicting this or that, denying the possibility of this or that, overlooking quite simple considerations. If Wordsworth had had no Coleridge to inspire him, and Coleridge no Dorothy to be inspired by (it may be held to be due to their inspiration that we owe the poetry of Wordsworth's great decade; but perhaps not); if Coleridge, still at the Blue Coat School, had been run over in Cheapside and killed; if Shelley and Keats had never been born, or had both died in infancy, what would the Histories of English Literature say of the poetry of the first quarter of last century? That it was a somewhat infertile period in England? For if there had been no Shelley in the person of Percy Bysshe, and no Keats in the person of John, there would have been no Shelley and Keats; for they were not persons produced by a Nature abhorring a vacuum in poetry, so that, if she did not produce those two poets, she must produce two others like them. Be it remarked further that, though there had been three men with Shelley's gift, and three men with Keats's, England would have been just as far as she was from possessing another Milton in 1825.

What Hazlitt said was true: the vividness of the impression in the poet's mind excites 'an involuntary movement of imagination and passion', producing 'by sympathy a certain modulation of the voice or sounds expressing it'. That the involuntary movement of imagination and passion, since it is sometimes produced, might be more often produced than not; in other words, that a man might be more likely to be a poet than not to be one, is what we might expect, except that we know by experience that the movement is very rarely produced. That is only to say:—except that we know that poets are rare. They *are* rare; and of those things that are rare, it is to be expected that at times there should be none; that there should be some in some places, and in others none. So at times there will be no poets; none, that is, whose work will endure. That is what is to be expected. But there being none at a given moment of time will not of itself have any influence in bringing it about that fifty years later there should still be none, or that there should then be two; just as there having been two fifty years before the supposed date had no connexion with there having been none at the date. The wind bloweth whither it listeth.

There is really nothing in what is happening to-day in the world of English poetry from which we can argue anything certain as to the future of English poetry. It is an incalculable field.

Even if the great poetry of one period led by some inevitable chain to there being poetry written in the next period, there would not at any date be the possibility of accurately judging of the poetry of the future; for the poetry of any time is not fully known until a later time, not until after twenty or more years. There might have been men writing in 1825 of the future of English poetry who had not read anything by Keats and Shelley to speak of, and very much less than the entire bulk of the best work of Wordsworth and Coleridge. So to-day who knows that those who write about the English poetry of to-day and the future, the Trevelyans, the Abercrombies, the

Muirs, and the others—who is certain that they have read deeply in the poetry of the men whom future generations will rank as the most important poets of this age, if there be any such hidden men? It is just possible that the critics have not read a line of their writings.

Can, then, nothing of profit ever be written of the future of poetry? There is something, we think; the present of poetry can be written about in a way to influence the poetry of the future for good. But the writing must be that of a man with a very deep understanding, if it is to influence poetry for good; for poetry, though one of those things that seem open to almost every man's understanding, is a thing seldom written about in a way to instruct any one. The ease with which it seems able to be understood may be what misleads men.

A Keats will urge a Shelley, in a letter, to load every rift with ore. Any fine poet-critic may note of another that his rifts are not all being loaded with ore. Any one is able to think of wrong roads that a poet-critic might see another poet as taking. If they may be called attention to in a private letter, that may be done too in a piece of public writing, not addressed to any one man, but to men generally.

Was it not Goethe who said that he would write the songs of the common people? That might be some one's text: he might argue, to the profit of the poets to come after him, that if a man is writing something clearly never to be under-stood of the common people, he is taking a wrong road. He would probably be right. The ex-pression of involuntary movements of imagina-tion and passion ought not, one would say, to be difficult of understanding even by the common people. What is difficult for them to understand is the expression of the movements of the intellect of men engaged in analysing or in metaphysical speculation. A man might call the attention of his fellows to the fact that the poetry of the time was too much turned away from the common people. He would be doing good.

Again, a poet-critic might be struck by the fact that contemporary poetry had been moving away from the expression that is song; that is, the ex-pression of movements of imagination and passion in words meant to be sung, or at least chanted. To set forth that theme (it has been done, but there might be a profit in its being done again) would be to influence the poetry of the day for good, and to influence the poetry of the future as a thing in-fluenced, often powerfully, by the poetry of the recent past.

Another matter for writing about, still an almost

unexplored field, is the part that a poet's wife,
children, friends, play in the production of his
work, and the part that the general public plays.
There are poems of Browning, to draw illustra-
tions of what I mean from him, that would never
have been written, had Browning never married,
and other poems that would have been different, if
his wife had been a different woman. A poem
may owe its existence to the fact that a child has
died. A poem written because a child had died
might be destroyed because the mother's sense
was hurt by a theme so sacred to the home being
made the matter of song, however beautiful. The
core of a poem might be something that one of
the poet's friends had said. The core of another
might be something that the poet had read in a
book that he might never have read, if he had not
had a reading friend. A poem might be written
because about that time a Jowett urged the poet
to write something. One remembers reading a
letter in which Jowett urged Tennyson to write
something, seeking to fire him by telling him of
Browning's then unpublished and perhaps un-
finished *Ring and the Book*. A poet might be
indebted for a poem to a friend's having revealed
to him some part of his or her nature. Many of the
best poems must have had such sources.

The more the matter is looked into, indeed, the greater will be seen to be the part played by others in the writing of any man's poetry. The part played by the general public is more difficult to see, as a thing having recognizable features, than is the part played by the man's wife, children, friends; but it must exist, and it may even be large. What effect on a poet's work may not a strong public tide of interest in things unimportant or unworthy have; what effect a strong tide of public interest in things vital and worthy? What may come, to the heightening or debasing of a man's work, from the nobility or ignobility of his contemporaries? That is an endless theme. How much, one may ask, of the *Divina Commedia* was not shaped, less by Dante's character than by the character of his age, and how much of Dante's mind that passed into the poem would not have been his mind, if the acts and minds of his contemporaries had been very different; if there had been no Pope that had made 'il gran rifiuto'; if Dante's mood had not been habitually one of anger and contempt and scorn, which it would not have been had his lot been to work, not with such men as he had had to work with, but with such as Saul of Tarsus and John and Mark?

It might almost be argued that in any poem the

poet's part was the lesser of the two parts into which it might be thought of as divided; parts corresponding to its two sources—those that had their spring in himself and those that had their spring outside him. The vividness of the impression, to quote Hazlitt again, excites an involuntary movement of imagination and passion. The impression, then, is one created by other persons or by things. That the movement is involuntary means that it is not of the poet's unaided raising.

There, then, is a theme that ought to engage the attention of those whose profession it is to study these matters. It is an endless theme, full of promise. In following it out, a critic-poet might be qualifying to be a leader of men to new and richer countries; such a leader as Mr. Havelock Ellis was thinking of, when he wrote:

'When I look into Sadger's lately published "Lehre von den Geschlechtsverirrungen," or indeed into almost any psycho-analytic book that is not English or American, but perhaps especially this of Sadger's, for it is so relentless and so precise, I seem to see a hand that is pointed towards an approaching new horizon of the human spirit. I am careful not to say that I see the new horizon itself. That only exists in my own mind, for these books are too pedestrian, too prosaic, too (as they used to say before "matter" was recognized as a poetic fiction) materialistic, for so large a gesture. Yet they really point the way towards the direction in which poets and prophets will raise the curtain that covers the new horizon. They are doing more, they are actually laying the foundations of the structure on which the poets and prophets will stand. They are even themselves revealing in one aspect the new vision of the human soul.'

If the matter really is as it appears to me to be, it is dimly seen that there is need of a new relation between men generally and the poets; for once seen that men's lives generally have an effect on the work of their poet-countrymen, and that men's relations with those particular poets with whom life brings them in contact have a possibly profound influence on their work, and certainly some influence, which would be a new way of looking at the matter, changes would follow; many old things would be revised. Countries have the governments they deserve, it is said; that is to say, they have the governments which they make? Have they also the poets that they make? Not that men can control the incalculable—whether there be poets, or be none—but, given that there are poets, that they make them, or greatly mar them? That is the question. Could one write:—'An ignoble age, as one could judge from reading its poetry alone'? Or:—'An age of at least one great poet, more nobly seconded by men generally than perhaps ever poet before'? There would be sense in both of these.

An actual question that might arise in such a changed outlook is whether in the poet's feeling that this or that article of current morality hinders his expression—whether there is not in that more than an indication that the article is bad. A daring question, but perhaps all the better for that. If this gift of poetry, so rarely allowed by God, is not some accident, undesigned, but is a gift from heaven, with heaven's reason for being so rare—if that is so, who, in so difficult a matter as morality, were a better innovator; who more likely finely to feel the value of the current code in this or that article? The world's book of poetry, read by any one with the intention of discovering if poets appear to have had changes in their valuing of moral things forced on them by the poems they wrote, in somewhat the way in which novelists have felt that their half-written books were taking the direction into their hands—the book so read does show that that appears. In the consciousness of the poets, beyond the point where we can read it, it must have been plainer that, if they had obstinately refused to modify some currently accepted article, this or that poem simply could not have been written. Not that they were always as brave as men as they were as poets. Witness Wordsworth.

The more interesting matter, however, is the question of the greater help that particular persons, by winning their own freedom, can be to poets; by winning such freedom as these words speak of: 'Ye shall know the truth, and the truth shall make you free.' All poetry resumes and expresses experience. The circumstances most narrowing, to my view, are those that restrict the poet's public experience to a life of verse-writing and nothing else, except perhaps feverish journalism, made sordid by an element of log-rolling possibly. Those are the most narrowing circumstances in general. But even more devastating might be the narrowness produced by the accident of a particular poet's personal relations; if no man ever shows him anything of his soul, nor any woman. W. H. Hudson's brother said to him once: 'Of all the persons I have known you are the one I have known least.' If a poet should have at the end to say as much of that one, or those few, from whom, if he was to draw a rich experience, he must draw it? One can see that as possible.

That is the great theme offered to the professional critic-poets. It is the greatest. How far some of them are from seeing it, or from seeing their subject in any other illuminating way, can be judged from this: that one of them, unreproved, or not gravely reproved, has said that, while the great output of personal lyrics, 'good, bad, and indifferent,' is certain to continue, there is no hope for lyrics on a larger scale. To pass over the depreciation implied of good personal lyrics—such make one of the greatest bodies of poetry existing —let it be said that what hope there is for lyrics on a larger scale is a thing that nobody knows anything about whatever. Nothing whatever. What was known of *The Hound of Heaven* the year before it was written? What was known of *La Belle Dame Sans Merci* before it was written? How can any one know of poems before they are written? Of what nature is the knowledge? To have any knowledge, it would be necessary to have a means of judging the mind of some poet unborn, a thing difficult enough to do of a living mind, or rather of many poets unborn. To think such a thought as that there is no hope 'for lyrics on a larger scale' is to show a lack of understanding of fundamentals.

Another critic-poet might say that there is an untilled field in comic poetry, or narrative, or say the like, hoping to stand and point successfully to some poet where he should go. That is not how help can be given. If a great comic poet, another Butler or a greater, is born, he will know of himself which road is his. The thing of importance is, he having seen and chosen it, to help him along it. In the many ways that still are, as I have said, to be explored, and in the many ways that have been. They have been, but it is work that must always be a-doing, for since the last pregnant study of, say, metaphor, the world has moved on under the impetus by still later men. The world may since have abandoned metaphor, or have corrupted it. The world will not be exactly where it was. Even if that were not so, if only the same thing could be said again in other words, let it be. Those later-said words might be read by those by whom the earlier, for this reason or that, had not been. How many young men may be put off reading their Arnold, or put from their best understanding of it, by the current fashionable habit of depreciation? The world does not always know its own peace.

What can be learned from the work of foreign poets, the book of which grows larger as increase of knowledge brings far countries nearer, as the East, the Far East—that has not been enough inquired into.

How few great poets there have been, and how

small a proportion of their total work is great, and worthy of the study of the learner—that is a matter hardly yet touched, from the habit that so easily grows upon men of praising the things amongst which our own work lies. How much could not be learned by a young man from a profound, enlightened study of the *Golden Treasury,* one in which should be set forth which are the poems that most certainly should have been left out of it, and why? There is a tendency to an almost indiscriminate eulogy of the poets of the canon proceeding from this,—that there are so many more professors of poetry or literature, men from whom books are expected, men who want to write books, but not always about the same old names. So at any moment the world may be asked to reconsider some second-rate reputation. An attempt is made to add another name to the canon of the great, those with whose work one must make oneself familiar. Lines are dragged out and praised that had been forgotten and rightly forgotten. No man could do his contemporaries a worse harm of its kind than that. It is to encourage them to fritter away their gift. Hundreds of lines that have been printed during the last twenty-five years in England would have been seen by the writers as not good enough to pass, if the critic-poets had written of the older men under a severer discipline. If a young man sees this or that leading critic of the day approving poor work in the writings of former days, how much more likely he will be to yield to his ever present temptation to think that his own weak things are good enough, and will pass. Such approving is witnessed daily.

DR. SAINTSBURY'S HERESY

SOME time after 1893, but not long after, Dr. Saintsbury, in a paper on Tennyson, delivered a judgement on poetry; and, as he reprinted it without change in 1923, it may be taken as his considered judgement, and as one that many are ready to accept. The judgement is as follows:

'It often makes people positively angry to be told that the greatest part, if not the whole, of the pleasure-giving appeal of poetry, lies in its sound rather than in its sense, or, to speak with extreme exactness, lies in the manner in which the sound conveys the sense. No "chain of extremely valuable thoughts" is poetry in itself: it only becomes poetry when it is conveyed with those charms of language, metre, rhyme, cadence, what not, which certain persons disdain.

'This being so, and the mere matter of all poetry—to wit, appearances of nature, and the thoughts and feelings of men—being unalterable, it follows that the difference between poet and poet will depend upon the manner of each in applying language, metre, rhyme, cadence, and what not, to this invariable material.'

The material, I should maintain, is not invariable, but is infinitely variable. Let us examine some poems, and see how variable the material is.

I will begin with Byron's *Elegy on Thyrza* as being as good a poem to take as any, and also because I once read praise of it in a lecture or article of Professor Elton's; one, I noted a little sadly, that did not speak a word of the fact that it is a poem containing expressions that could have been uttered only by a man whose thought of all women matched what we know of Byron's intercourse with particular women.

I will not ask where thou liest low,
    Nor gaze upon the spot;
There flowers or weeds at will may grow,
    So I behold them not:
It is enough for me to prove
That what I loved, and long must love,
    Like common earth can rot:
To me there needs no stone to tell
'Tis nothing that I loved so well.

The flower in ripened bloom unmatched
    Must fall the earlier prey;
Though by no hand untimely snatched,
    The leaves must drop away.
And yet it were a greater grief
To watch it withering, leaf by leaf,
    Than see it plucked to-day;
Since earthly eye but ill can bear
To trace the change to foul from fair.

I know not if I could have borne
    To see thy beauties fade;
The night that followed such a morn
    Had worn a deeper shade:

Thy day without a cloud hath passed,
And thou wert lovely to the last,
 Extinguished, not decayed;
As stars that shoot along the sky
Shine brightest as they fall from high.

Contrast that poem, the utterance of a man to whom a woman (it sounds harsh to say so, but it is true) was a good bed-fellow, or was no longer one, with such a poem as:

Once . . . once upon a time . . .
 Over and over again,
Martha would tell us her stories,
 In the hazel glen.

Hers were those clear grey eyes
 You watch, and the story seems
Told by their beautifulness
 Tranquil as dreams.

She would sit with her two slim hands
 Clasped round her bended knees;
While we on our elbows lolled,
 And stared at ease.

Her voice, her narrow chin,
 Her grave small lovely head,
Seemed half the meaning
 Of the words she said.
      (Walter de la Mare.)

or with:

Fast—fast asleep; her two hands held
 Loose folded on her knee,

So that her small unconscious face
    Looked half unreal to me;
So calmly lit with sleep's pale light
    Each feature was; so fair
Her forehead—every trouble was
    Smoothed out beneath her hair.
                    (*Walter de la Mare.*)

Both of those are pictures of old women's faces.
To many a man's mind old faces will come more
readily than young, and come fuller, not only of
meaning and pathos, but of charm and sheer
beauty. But they come only to those who have
eyes to see. Of all the faces that I passed in the
streets, my last furlough in London, I can now,
three years later, recall only one; the face of a little
lady whose hair was white almost as snow.

Contrast Byron's poem with such as:

She lived unknown, and few could know
    When Lucy ceased to be;
But she is in her grave, and, oh,
    The difference to me.

    .   .   .   .

How well I know what I mean to do
    When the long dark autumn evenings come;
And where, my soul, is thy pleasant hue?
    With the music of all thy voices, dumb
In life's November too!

And to watch you sink by the fire-side now
    Back again, as you mutely sit
Musing by fire-light, that great brow
    And the spirit-small hand propping it,
Yonder, my heart knows how!

So, earth has gained by one man the more,
    And the gain of earth must be heaven's gain too;
And the whole is well worth thinking o'er
    When autumn comes: which I mean to do
One day as I said before.

Contrast Byron's poem, with the dreadful declaration that he would rather young life was snatched away, for

        it were a greater grief
    To watch it withering, leaf by leaf,
        Than see it plucked to-day;
        Since earthly eye but ill can bear
        To trace the change to foul from fair—

one protests: life does not grow from fair to foul; not a flower, not a rose, not a leaf, not a human face: there is beauty in every season—contrast that poem of Byron's, and all his poetry about women, with the possible exception of the poem about the lady

        Who walks in beauty like the night
        Of cloudless climes and starry skies,

and you will know beyond question that Mr. De la Mare and Wordsworth and very specially

Browning could have had no ease of mind in talking with Byron about women; which is as much as
to say that the material of poetry, as far as women
make it, was one thing to him and an utterly
different thing to them. He saw what he saw, and
they saw what they saw; and still Another would
have seen what He would have seen.

So all poetry shows. What makes the little really
great poetry that the world possesses the great
poetry that it is (is it not, too, a far smaller body
than the professors think?) is that the material
was in the possession of only those few men. To
the rest of mankind it was a sealed book.

I propose to say nothing more for the present
about Dr. Saintsbury's invariableness of the
material, but to place passages side by side, and
try to make clearer, at least to myself, in what the
great poetry differs from all the rest.

> Far from the madding crowd's ignoble strife
> Their sober wishes never learned to stray;
> Along the cool sequestered vale of life
> They kept the noiseless tenour of their way.
> Yet e'en these bones from insult to protect
> Some frail memorial still erected high,
> With uncouth rhymes and shapeless sculpture decked,
> Implores the passing tribute of a sigh—

that is seen not to be great poetry, for one can

without difficulty imagine some other contemplative man, if led into a country churchyard and asked to think of it as a subject of a poem—one can easily imagine him thinking very much the same thoughts as Gray's. I do not mean a man too far removed in space or time.

> How happy is he born and taught
> That serveth not another's will;
> Whose armour is his honest thought
> And simple truth his utmost skill—

for that coin, one feels, the poet dipped into a pretty common purse.

> Lift not thy spear against the Muse's bower—

yes, certainly, that might have been another man's thought.

> The great Emathian conqueror bid spare
> The house of Pindarus, when temple and tower
> Went to the ground: and the repeated air
> Of sad Electra's poet had the power
> To save the Athenian walls from ruin bare—

yes, that too another man might have thought out, if 'the repeated air' is very near the door that is closed upon us all, or is behind that door. There is the purest poetry of speech in it as distinguished from the poetry of thought.

> . . . when we hope to find,
> And think to burst out into sudden blaze,

Comes the blind *Fury* with th'abhorred shears,
And slits the thin spun life.

It was that fatall and perfidious Bark
Built in th'eclipse, and rigg'd with curses dark,
That sunk so low that sacred head of thine.

              his Bonnet sedge,
Inwrought with figures dim, and on the edge
Like to that sanguine flower inscrib'd with woe.

        though I have lost
Much lustre of my native brightness, lost
To be belov'd of God,

        Satan bowing low
His grey dissimulation, disappear'd
Into thin air diffus'd:

all those are most certainly behind the eternally
shut door. We can think of no man but Milton,
or another having equal genius, having such
thoughts, and so expressing them. It is in the hope
of finding things like those, some such flashes and
revelation and glory, that one reads volume upon
volume of poetry.

I cannot tell what flowers are at my feet,
   Nor what soft incense hangs upon the boughs,
But, in embalmed darkness, guess each sweet
   Wherewith the seasonable month endows
The grass, the thicket, and the fruit-trees wild:
   White hawthorn, and the pastoral eglantine:

> Fast fading violets covered up in leaves;
>   And mid-May's eldest child,
> The coming musk-rose, full of dewy wine,
> The murmurous haunt of flies on summer eves—

that does not thrill a man: we feel that, give us but a moderate gift of verse-writing, or a little more than the gift that has been given, and we might write something not unlike that; at least that we might quite well have the same thoughts.

> Thou wast not born for death, immortal bird.
>   No hungry generations tread thee down;
> The voice I hear this passing night was heard
>   In ancient days by emperor and clown—

that, too, but with far greater labour, we might have written. But with:

> Perhaps the self-same song that found a path
>   Through the sad heart of Ruth, when, sick for home,
>   She stood in tears amid the alien corn;

> Sometimes whoever seeks abroad may find
> Thee sitting careless on a granary floor,
> Thy hair soft-lifted by the winnowing wind.

> Now more than ever seems it rich to die,
>   To cease upon the midnight with no pain.

> Forlorn! the very word is like a bell
>   To toll me back from thee to my sole self!

>   unheard
> Save of the quiet Primrose, and the span

Of heaven and few ears,
Rounded by thee, my song should die away
Content as theirs,
Rich in the simple worship of a day.

St. Agnes' Eve—Ah, bitter chill it was!
The owl, for all his feathers, was a-cold;
The hare limp'd trembling through the frozen grass,
And silent was the flock in woolly fold:

And they are gone: aye, ages long ago
These lovers fled away into the storm.

                               there shall be
Beautiful things made new, for the surprise
Of the sky-children; I will give command.

Until at length old Saturn lifted up
His faded eyes, and saw his kingdom gone,
And all the gloom and sorrow of the place—

with all those the door is flung wide open; for no man but Keats could have written them. If he had never lived, then the world would have been created, and again uncreated, without those words.

Mr. Havelock Ellis wrote one June day: 'It seemed to me that man, who in the Neolithic Age had discovered the uses of Corn and begun to make Bread, had not at first divined all the Eleusinian significance of that Mystery, but had in a later age sent Keats to the Earth in order to show that in the delight of the sensory physical things of the world is also to be found an exalted imaginative quality of the spirit, standing in the mere cornfield, a Ruth to announce higher things.'

Just so, and that was Keats's material. Whose was it before it was his?

A writer on Marlowe, Miss Ellis-Fermor, has: 'When rapture touches him he is, as to the language of the senses, speechless, except for an image or two. He cannot give direct utterance to an emotion or an impression made upon his senses, because that is not the habit of his thought. He may, perhaps, succeed in touching upon accompanying emotions or images, but it is in the world of the ideas that lie behind these outward forms that he moves familiarly, and in the almost mystic utterance of the spirit itself that his wealth lies.'

Just so again, and that was Marlowe's material. When all men, or at least all poets, have an equal insight into all things, it will be time to say that the material of poetry is invariable. Until then we may listen to a Tennyson speaking of himself, saying, 'To be sure, I've got nothing to say.'

Or take this little poem, called *To Delia*, the name of the writer of which I have a reason for withholding:

Notes of bell, and beech-tree green, and starlight
Make her voice, and dress, and skin.

Ringing bells, and scent of thyme, and blood-red
Poppies nodding to a tune within
Honeysuckled, wild-rose hedged-in meadows
Call her darling: and the shame
And the darkness of her absence
Make her hair and name.

May it not be said of that that it could only have
been written in the twentieth century; that it
needed a general growth of the mind of Englishmen in certain directions for any one of them to
have such thoughts? Might not that, too, be
said of the greater number of the poems of any
significance, written since the century began? If I
have not by this time made my point, however,
I shall never make it.

WALT WHITMAN

I HAVE been trying to make out what kind of man Walt Whitman really was, and the physiognomy of his life. I have always supposed that he was christened 'Walt'. He was not christened 'Walt'; he was christened 'Walter'; but 'Walter Whitman' sounds absurd. The first thing to do, then, is to forget that he was Walter; to remember him as Walt, a pioneer. He was that even in clothes: he wore a red flannel shirt, open at the neck, and it was long ago, when Count D'Orsay was still showing how a dandy could dress who gave his mind to it; long before Almond of Loretto, that genius of a British schoolmaster, began to undermine British dress.

Whitman seems to have divided his life between crowds and solitude, which is what every poet should do; for only in the crowd is the experience to be gained without which a man, even a Tennyson, will have 'nothing to say', and only in solitude can he learn to know himself; can he know what it is to be a chosen vessel. The chosen vessel is never shaped in a crowd. Whitman sought crowds in theatres, ferry boats, in streets and through the columns of the newspapers that he helped to write; newspapers that he wrote with a most sensitive apprehension of the presence of the persons who were his readers. He sought solitude in woods and fields, or wherever it could be found. It could be found even in a ferry boat, if you turned your back on the people, and stood leaning over the side, half-watching the water. Whitman would do that. When he was twenty, when he was teaching school, as the Americans say, he was living in Jamaica (not the island, but a little town of that name not far from New York) with a family called Brenton, the head of which he helped to bring out the *Long Island Democrat*; but he was to be longer remembered in that household for loafing on his back under the apple-trees, looking up at the sun, than for his work on the newspaper. He was then making experience of himself, and of the roots in the under-world.

What he had to learn that it was most important that he should learn was how to live more largely than common men do; to learn to live as they cannot, because the doors to their subconscious minds are all shut, or because the convolutions of the grey-matter of their brains are inadequate, or whatever the obstacle is: nobody knows what it is. Whitman could only learn to live largely by listening to his own instincts and emotions, feeling for

them, sublimating them, or flinging them the
reins. He must deepen what we call the imagination, not really knowing what it is, or how better
to call it. That can only be done in solitude, and
loafing under apple-trees is solitude.

The portrait, the only one I have seen, of Whitman's father, once a farmer, afterwards a house
builder, when farming had failed with him, shows
the anxious face and untidy hair of a confused,
unsuccessful man, which appears to have been
what he was, but still a man who might have a son
with his father's sensitiveness; and, if there was
a mother to add'grit—and Walt Whitman's mother
was Dutch, and bore sons and daughters, and they
loved her—the son might succeed in that in which
the father had failed. One of Whitman's bio-
graphers has this: 'The stranger meeting the
large, rough figure of Whitman . . . would not
have suspected that his body was probably the
most sensitive in the city, his sense of hearing and
smell exceptionally acute, and his touch so highly
developed, that personal force went out of him at
each contact of the hand with properly sensitive
hands.' Whitman himself wrote:

Mine is no callous shell,
I have instant conductors all over me whether I pass or stop,
They seize every object and lead it harmlessly through me.

That was one of the discoveries of solitude—that life, all of it, would pass through any so single a being harmlessly.

Whitman, they say, had a genius for friendship, and it is seen to have grown more powerful as he matured. The friendship he offered men and women—it is a thing as much worth study as his book is—was akin to the feeling that man has for nature, a feeling impartial, receptive, kindly, uncritical, like that of an open-eyed child. He was never tired by the repetition of the same sight, human or natural. He never tired of the sights of the streets. Those were the days of the omnibus in New York. There were so many of them, that it has been said that it would have been possible to walk on the tops of them from the Astor house to Wall Street. They were handsome stages, drawn by two or four horses, and brightly painted. I have all this from Mr. Emory Holloway's *Whitman: An Interpretation in Narrative*, a book to which I am indebted for many other things. You got in at the side or at the back of the omnibus, and passed up your fare to the driver through a hole in the roof. There was a second seat on the box, and that was where Whitman always sat. No inside for that nature-loving man, inured to the sun and all weathers. Whitman knew all the

buses, and all their drivers. At first they were
a little suspicious of him, because he knew so
much of the insides of books, but when one winter,
a driver lying ill, Whitman took his place, and
drove the bus to support the man's family, the
confraternity opened their hearts to him.

Whitman would be standing at the curb, and
a driver, seeing him, would draw up, and would
cast at him a friendly and inquiring glance.
Whitman, if he was so minded, would seize the
handle without a word (what handle? the handle
of the driver's whip?), and swing up with a spring-
ing, elastic motion to the off-side of the box, 'as
quietly', he put it, 'as a hawk swoops to its nest'.
The wheels were iron-shod, and the streets were
paved with cobbles: against that din no voice could
carry far. Up there would sit this new kind of
man, new but linked in spirit to older men, for
he might presently be shouting lines from Homer
or out of a play of Shakespeare. Or he would be
listening to the stories or life-history of the driver,
not forgetting, however, to salute four out of five
of the drivers that they passed.

Once, when one of the drivers died, not an old
man, Whitman wrote a requiem, and this is part of it:

He was a good fellow, free-mouthed, quick-tempered, not
bad-looking,

Ready with life or death for a friend, fond of women,
gambled, ate hearty, drank hearty,
Had known what it was to be flush, grew low-spirited
toward the last, sickened, was helped by a contribution,
Died, aged forty-one years—and that was his funeral.

Thumb extended, finger uplifted, apron, cape, gloves,
strap, wet-weather clothes, whip carefully chosen,
Boss, spotter, starter, hostler, somebody loafing on you,
you loafing on somebody, headway, man before and
man behind,
Good day's work, bad day's work, pet stock, mean stock,
first out, last out, turning-in at night,
To think that these are so much and so nigh to other
drivers, and he there takes no interest in them.

Whitman was once inside a car. Pete Doyle, an
Irishman, the car conductor, a friend of Whitman
from the day described until the end, tells the
story.

'He was the only passenger, it was a lonely night, so I
thought I would go in and talk with him. Something in me
made me do it and something in him drew me that way.
He used to say there was something in me had the same
effect on him.'

Men who in solitude have drunk the milk of
paradise have that effect on other men. This that
follows is from some papers entrusted to me. The
writer's language, as will be clearly seen, is not

English. He is of Hungary and Budapest, but is writing to an Englishman:

'I don't know how and why it is, that since I saw you the first time in my life that you appeared to me as familiar as my own brother. Why? Can you give a plausible explanation? I think, once I already put before you this question. You left it unanswered. Try to reply it.'

The answers to such questions may be what they may be; they are never of the kind that we call plausible.

Whitman, in a relation with Pete Doyle or whoever it might be, had something of the feeling of a lover, and got something of the feeling of the lover in return. He counted such friendships by the score, however, and numbers in such a matter make for health and purity. In any case he was to let all life flow through him. Men had won freedom from tyrants and their Star Chambers and other instruments, but to Whitman, in a wild wood or on a sea-beach, that had seemed only the beginning of freedom, with the rest all to win. If he was a pioneer, it was in the world of the freedom of man's spirit; release from the other world, the one in which it could be asked:

> Is it a party in a parlour,
> Crammed just as they on earth were crammed;
> Some sipping punch, some sipping tea,
> But as you by their faces see,
> All silent and all damned?

was still to be won. Whatever there might be for joy to Pete Doyle and himself there must be, or he was not free. That was plain enough to see.

The imprint of the countryside in which such a man as Whitman grows up will be on his spirit. The countryside in which Whitman did grow up was for the most part a plain, covered with kill-calf, huckleberry bushes, with pasture for hundreds of milch cows. The clanking of copper cowbells, as the cattle filed homeward of an evening, would be one of the familiar sounds. The farther east, the worse the country looks; scrub oak and pine everywhere, and among them, when darkness comes on, the fires of the charcoal burners light up. Roads there are here and there, along some of which Whitman once rode on a pony on Saturdays, delivering the first newspaper of his editing to the subscribers. Ten or fifteen years later, the South having meanwhile been seen, and some woman of the South loved and known, his mind suddenly grew mature, and then he had other things to do than to edit newspapers, and ride the country roads on a pony, delivering them.

He wrote:

I believe in you my soul, the other I am must not abase
  itself to you,

And you must not be abased to the other.

* * * * * *

Swiftly arose and spread around me the peace and know-
ledge that pass all the argument of the earth,
And I know that the hand of God is the promise of my
own,
And I know that the spirit of God is the brother of my
own,
And that all the men ever born are also my brothers, and
the women my sisters and lovers,
And that a kelson of the creation is love,
And limitless are leaves stiff or drooping in the fields,
And brown ants in the little wells beneath them,
And mossy scabs of the worn fence, heap'd stones, elder,
mullein and poke-weed,

'Kelson' or 'keelson', if I may tell those who do
not know, and have not guessed, is the name they
give to the line of timber that fastens a ship's floor-
timbers to the keel. There would need to be a
kelson in creation, love or another; and the mission
of the best of each generation is to rediscover, and
tell men what it is. The knowledge may come in
a flash, but it will have had springs long fed; and
part of the feeding may even be half a life of
watching leaves, stiff or drooping in the fields, and
the ants in the little wells beneath them, and mossy
scabs on fences, and heaped stones, and the mark-
ings on stones. A man may spend half a life watching

such things, with no certainty, for how could there be any? of good to come of it; he sustained by a hope to which he puts no words. Some inner voice tells him in the silence that he also is a poet or seer.

Browning prepared to write a poem on the risen Lazarus, asking himself how such a one would react to things; as we ordinary men do? not as we do? Then he makes Karshish, the Arab physician into whose mouth he puts it all—he makes him say, after asking his audience to think of a beggar to whom a sudden wealth has come:

> So here—we call the treasure knowledge, say,
> Increased beyond the fleshly faculty—
> Heaven opened to a soul while yet on earth,
> Earth forced on a soul's use while seeing heaven;
> The man is witless of the size, the sum,
> The value in proportion of all things,
> Or whether it be little or be much.
> Discourse to him of prodigious armaments
> Assembled to besiege his city now,
> And of the passing of a mule with gourds—
> 'Tis one! Then take it on the other side,
> Speak of some trifling fact,—he will gaze rapt
> With stupor at its very littleness,
> (Far as I see) as if in that indeed
> He caught prodigious import, whole results;
> And so will turn to us the bystanders
> In ever the same stupor (note this point)
> That we too see not with his opened eyes.

Whitman was such a Lazarus. When his mind
matured at last, it was as if he had died, and had
seen heaven. He had afterwards earth's use thrust
upon him while seeing heaven. Had he not had
the apprehension of the omnibus drivers, the ferry-
men, the crowds in the theatres, the readers of
newspapers, as the men who would read his poems;
had he not had the wish to write something intelligible to them, something to give them a larger life
to live, one doubts if he would have written a word
for any one to understand literally. Does any poet
want to write such words? It is doubtful. Would
they not all rather write such words as:

> Full fathom five thy father lies:
> Of his bones are coral made;
> Those are pearls that were his eyes:
> Nothing of him that doth fade,
> But doth suffer a sea-change
> Into something rich and strange.
> Sea-nymphs hourly ring his knell:
> Hark! now I hear them,—
> Ding, dong, bell.

One knows the circular patches of lichen that
grow on old stones in a wall, or as they lie on the
ground. There is more for a Whitman's thought in
them than there is in any triumph of an Austerlitz
battle. Wordsworth once waited, watching for the
led palfrey on which he was to ride home at the

beginning of one of the school vacations,—he watched, half-sheltered by a naked wall, with a sheep couched on one hand, and a blasted haw- thorn standing on the other. Years afterwards he could write of them so that the lines have a haunt- ingness in them, a something that might dwell in the mind when almost all the rest of the 'Prelude' was forgotten; such was the measure of the differ- ence between the way these men react to such things and the way we do.

> . . . afterwards, the wind and sleety rain,
> And all the business of the elements,
> The single sheep, and the one blasted tree,
> And the bleak music from that old stone wall,
> The noise of wind and water, and the mist . . .

That is about as near, I believe, as one can get to understanding how things worked in Whit- man's mind;—to see him as having a mystic's sense of the significance of things, joined to any common man's abundant or superabundant interest in the men and things surrounding him. When an Exhibition (it was in 1853) was opened in New York, Whitman began his visits to it, and he kept them up a whole year. So persistent was he in his study of whatever interested him deeply, that his figure excited the suspicions of the police. He would stand for hours, gazing at Thorwaldsen's

marbles, he, a rough-looking, plainly dressed man.
Of course the police thought he could be up to no
good. One of the photographs of him shows him
as looking like a tramp—beard of the shaggiest
and untidiest—as any man not a tramp could look.

If he did not write the fully revealing poetry
that he meant to write, the poetry which should
reveal man's estate to men, well he knew what it
should be. Listen to him:

'Here comes one among the well-beloved stone-cutters,
and announces himself, and plans with decision and science,
and sees the solid and beautiful forms of the future where
there are now no solid forms. . . . His rhythm and unifor-
mity he will conceal in the roots of his verses, not to be seen
of themselves, but to break forth loosely as lilacs on a bush,
or take shapes compact, as the shapes of melons, or chest-
nuts, or pears.'

RICHARD MIDDLETON

Dear God, what means a poet more or less?

RICHARD MIDDLETON wrote that. He was of our time; had he not died as a young man (he was only twenty-nine), he would still be alive. He belongs to that group of latter-day English poets—Ernest Dowson, Lionel Johnson, John Davidson, and Stephen Phillips—who, if they have not this or that in common, have all of them this, that they, dying young, added their names to those others who died young; the roll, the chief names in which are Chatterton and Keats. A roll to which one may add Shelley's name, though his was a violent death, and the names of those whom the Great War took away; the last, in their fate, more fortunate, perhaps, than the others. One broods over the long list of names until one can hardly bear to think of the men any longer. What went so wrong with them? Why should Milton, Goethe, Wordsworth, Tennyson, Browning have proved so much tougher? There is perhaps a key to the mystery in a phrase in one of Richard Middleton's last letters:—'I feel drawn towards young children and people who are simple and kindly and not too clever. They give me a glimpse

of the life that I have missed in my passionate
search for enjoyment.'

One expects a poet to want to enjoy life, and life
within rather narrow limits, and one sees that they
do set out to seek enjoyment; but they mostly
burn themselves out too soon. What keeps those
from burning themselves out who do not do so is,
I believe, this; that they care more for poetry, for
the poetry that they feel they must live to write.
One feels that Milton or Wordsworth would as
soon have gone so far in their search for enjoyment
as to incapacitate themselves for writing more
poetry, as an austere priest would take the lamb
from the altar, and give it to the pigs. There must
be, for a man to be a great poet, and to fulfil his
destiny, some cold principle in him of self-
reservation; something almost like cynical calcula-
tion. Wordsworth would go only so far with his
French Annette as would not prevent his writing:

Thou dost preserve the stars from wrong,
And the most ancient heavens through thee are fresh and
strong.

One sees the self-reservation working most plainly
in Goethe, the Goethe of whom John Sterling and
Carlyle could write as this letter shows:

'Truly, as you say, one might ask the question, whether
anybody did love this man, as friend does friend; especially,

Whether this man did ever frankly love anybody? I think in one sense, it is very likely the answer were No to both questions; and yet, in another sense, how emphatically Yes! Few had a right to "love" this man, except in the way you mention: nay, what living man had? Schiller, perhaps to some extent; and accordingly Schiller did, to something like that extent. One does not love the Heaven's lightning, in the way of caresses altogether! This man's love, I take it, lay deep-hidden in him, as fire in the earth's centre; at the surface,—since he could not be a Napoleon, did not like to be a broken, self-consumed Burns,—what could it do for him?

'The earliest instincts of self-culture, I suppose, and all the wider insights he got in the course of that, would alike prescribe for him: Hide all this, renounce all this; all this leads to madness, indignity, Rousseauism, and will forever remain bemocked, ignominiously crucified one way or the other, in this lower earth: let thy love, far hidden, spring up as a soul of beauty, and be itself victorious, beautiful.'

The consuming eroticism of the cold North— I think one has to have lived in such a country as India to see it for what it is. It speaks in Middleton's poetry more than anything else. It is young at first; a wine, not yet a poison, and so there is a loveliness, as in this poem:

New Love

The boy weeps in the wild woods,
His bright eyes are sore,

The old inhuman solitudes
  May shield his heart no more;
A maid has happened out of hell
And kissed his crimson lips too well.

Where may he hide his miseries?
  Where quench the lips that burn
For scarlet love? the tangled trees,
  Bramble and gorse and fern
Can hide him not, nor may he cool
His mouth in any forest pool.

Love laughs about the groves of pine,
  Pan wantons in the glade,
And the boy is drunk with a new wine,
  And the boy's heart is afraid;
Her lips were soft and very kind,
Her breath was like a summer wind.

Oh! wanton night, made glad with dew,
  Hung with a starry veil!
The boy is lost for loving you,
  The old enchantments fail.
You have led his feet to hell's gate—
To a crimson dawn and passionate.

No more in leafy solitudes,
  God's paved fields among,
He shall win the peace of the wild woods
  With the joy of his quiet song.
For love has found the groves of pine,
And the boy is drunk with a new wine.

There is not much sign of self-reservation in that. The maid would resent self-reservation? Very possibly, but if great poetry is to be written, or even less than great, many things must be done, I believe, that a maid would resent. I should be the last to throw stones. Seeing that we none of us know why God put it into the heart of man to be poet, *Dichter*, whether in word, stone, colour, or sound, and know as little what good or evil there is in all men's part in poetry, what it will all have amounted to before the world is done, we may be of an open mind as to the morality of any man's search for his revelation. There are moments when it seems as if the failure of most artistry of the past sprang, not from the artists' immorality, but from their morality; or as if their art had really been born in a world in which there was neither, and suffered from having to be translated into the terms of a world in which both, alas, abound. But perhaps that is fanciful.

To go back to that poem. Poor Middleton, if his eroticism had not so filled his ear, he would have heard in his own words:

> the tangled trees,
> Bramble and gorse and fern,

and the music of them, something better to follow than his 'passionate search for enjoyment'. That

is how it works with the self-reserved: they hear in
their own music sweeter voices and better to follow
than the voices of the sirens. But theirs is a dog's
life—brooding everlastingly over the earth and the
dusty ground, in the hope that a flower of poetry
will peep through; brooding alone and silently.

Middleton went his own way, and one cannot
say that he did not find things to justify him.
They happen not to be the things that I care for
most myself, and those I do care for most do not
kill a man before he is thirty. This is part of a
poem called *To Irene*:

I think the earth was dead last night, for I,
    Keeping you in my arms, could feel no breath
    From all the slumbrous trees, it seemed that death
Had wooed the fields, for in our ecstasy
They had no part and where the thrushes flew
    In drowsy autumn, now no creature moved
    Across the fallen leaves, save where we loved,
And there I heard faint wings discover you.

And then you thrilled with some supreme desire
    That was not of my dreams, your pulses beat
    Time to the world, and with rebellious feet
Your triumphing passions scaled the gates of fire;
And lo, I was as dust! in some far place
    My soul paid tribute to tremendous kings,
    Who bowed their head before your gleaming wings
And praised your beauty with averted face.

There is nothing as weak in that as:

> Oh! wanton night made glad with dew,
> Hung with a starry veil!

and other weak things in *New Love*, which it must be confessed grows steadily weaker as it moves from the inspiration with which it began; if there is nothing as weak, nothing as hackneyed and commonplace, the poem has a graver fault. What does it mean? What multitude of people, in a world already so full of beautiful poetry, can be thought of as being moved to cherish in their hearts lines with features no clearer than:

> no creature moved
> Across the fallen leaves, save where we loved,
> And there I heard faint wings discover you?

The features of this, in a piece called *The Bathing Boy*, are clearer:

> Till with a sudden grace of silver skin
>   And golden lock he dived, his song of joy
> Broke with the bubbles as he bore them in;
>   And lo, the fear of night was on that place,
>   Till decked with new-found gems and flushed of face,
> He rose again, a laughing, choking boy.

The copy in which I have read Middleton's poems belongs to an Indian friend. He has starred two of the poems in pencil, and I take them to be the poems that have appealed most to him.

They are *Lullaby* and *On a Dead Child*. I cannot bring myself to repeat the first: it is too much the same lullaby that we have heard before many times. This is *On a Dead Child*:

Man proposes, God in His time disposes,
　　And so I wandered up to where you lay,
A little rose among the little roses,
　　And no more dead than they.

It seemed your childish feet were tired of straying,
　　You did not greet me from your flower-strewn bed,
Yet still I knew that you were only playing—
　　Playing at being dead.

I might have thought that you were really sleeping,
　　So quiet lay your eyelids to the sky,
So still your hair, but surely you were peeping,
　　And so I did not cry.

God knows, and in His proper time disposes,
　　And so I smiled and gently called your name,
Added my rose to your sweet heap of roses,
　　And left you to your game.

It cannot have been Middleton's own child, and the man to whom the poem appealed so much cannot ever have lost a child. The loss of a man's own child is of all human experiences the very ghastliest.

DR. EDWARD THOMPSON'S
POETRY

HAVING ventured to say that what is wrong with present-day criticism of poetry (it is what has always been wrong with contemporary criticism) is that it is written by men who have not read their authors carefully enough, and for people who will not do that either; further that, in a perfectly organized republic of letters, one critic would be told off to study each writer, so that each should be studied adequately, I may be said to have laid upon myself the task of studying one writer. At any rate I have done that, and this is the result. The poet whose work I have studied is Dr. Edward Thompson, a man better known, perhaps, as a critic and prose writer; but he is a poet also. He has several volumes of poetry to his credit, but I believe they have been read by very few.

One thing that stands in the way of recognition of the poetry of any new poet, but the chief is that men will not spend time enough in reading it, is the excess of attention that the Ancients exact. The appearance of a reprint of Greene, Marlowe, Marvell, Vaughan, Donne, or who it may be, sets twenty critics writing about Greene, Marlowe, Marvell, Vaughan, or Donne; though obviously, unless the critic has given some year or more of study to the Ancient, he cannot have anything to say about him that has not often been said already. I have just come from reading a page on Donne by a leading English critic. It is a page of praise of Donne that no man would have written, if moved in his own spirit to write of Donne, and not moved merely by the appearance in the book market of a reprint of Donne; if in his spirit had blossomed some flower of understanding of that Ancient. The critic quotes:

But Oh, too common.ill, I brought with mee
That, which betray'd mee to my enemie:
A loud perfume, which at my entrance cried
Even at thy father's nose, so we were spied.
When, like a tyran king, that in his bed
Smelt gunpowder, the pale wretch shivered.
Had it been some bad smell, he would have thought
That his owne feet, or breath, that smell had wrought;

but does not go on to assure us, as surely he might have done, that, in a world in which so much has been written since, nobody need trouble to read that, but regrets the omission of the poem (*The Perfume*) from the reprint. 'There is a great deal of poetry in the world not worth reading,' says

Professor Garrod at the beginning of his *Keats*. There is indeed.

It was of the essence of my plan that the poet whom I should study should be an unrecognized man; so my choice of Dr. Thompson requires no explanation. Any other unknown contemporary poet would have served my purpose, which was to perform once, for my part, the act of justice due to each writer, and to show, as well as I could, the judging of a poet so far unjudged. The judging, it will be obvious, could not always be done in public; consideration both for the writer judged and for the public would sometimes forbid. Dr. Thompson has had a sufficiently adequate experience of life to make it probable that his poetry is worth reading. It shows (not a little of it was written after the age at which those who are poets only in their youth leave off writing) that he has a healthy mind in a healthy body; that he has known nature, man, and work; that he has taught; that he has been responsible for numbers; that he has travelled; that he has read; that he has thought. He has loved and suffered. If one was dealing with a known poet, one would either pass over such matters altogether, or refer to them only when some poem could not be fully understood without some such reference; or so one might think; but

a book on the poetry of, say, Wordsworth, or
indeed any poet, is as a rule always as much about
the man as about his poetry. When the question is
whether a man should be read at all, the knowledge
of what his life has been, so far as it can then be
known, may be decisive. In addition to all the rest,
Dr. Thompson had a long and varied experience
during the War. He has kept, too, some hold on
the faith of his fathers. He has clearly succeeded
in many things: it is improbable that his poetry
should be of no value: he declares his own sense of
its value by publishing it.

If posterity should think that Dr. Thompson
has written great poetry, in which of his poems it
is will be more certainly known then than can
possibly be known to-day. The contemporary
praise of any real poet is always afterwards felt to
have been as faint-hearted as the contemporary
over-praise of the easy favourite of the day is afterwards felt to have been absurd. That is a thing for
no critic ever to forget. The great triumph of
a critic is to come as near the judgement of posterity as is humanly possible. I doubt myself if
Dr. Thompson has written the poetry that I see
as belonging to the highest, the poetry in which
the secret of things is revealed by their being
shown in the light of other things. He comes very

near it often: it is certainly his manner. One feels he would sometimes have reached it, if he had brooded a little longer; even if it had been more deeply known to his generation that without metaphor poetry has only half her voice. There are poems of his that are in the vein of reflection or emotion without imagery; but when he is most himself, his mind naturally thinks in images. The following is a poem about the Indian banian, the fruits of which, large but not bright red berries, though many be scattered on the ground, crowd the tree, the vastness of which is its so well-known feature:

Now for their winter feast
In the banian boughs joy-tremulous guests are shrilling;
The tree is a laurelled priest,
His old palms spreading, the air with blessing filling.
The winds fly forth from his hands,
And wide through the ways his benedictions scatter—
'Lo,' they cry, 'where he stands,
Offering fruits, four on each four-leaved platter.'

Another poem of imagery is:

This ancient thorn now like a beggar stands,
Thrusting through tattered sleeves its agued hands
That shake to the chill breeze, a mendicant
For such poor boon as niggard skies will grant. . . .
Yet still one branch survives; and still, with Spring,
Life will flood back to this dead, dreaming thing,

The swelling sap will rise, the old delight
Wrap up one wrinkled arm with blossomed white.

Dr. Thompson may owe 'mendicant', 'boon', and
'niggard' to his reading (there are at any moment
words that are just passing out of the richest life
of speech; words like flowers that have been just
an hour or two too long in the bowl on the table);
but in

Thrusting through tattered sleeves its agued hands

and

Wrap up one wrinkled arm with blossomed white

he is himself. There is only needed, as I feel
things, some deeper love or pity to make a melody,
a music, of words, to ensure that the lines would
reverberate in us (verse is not poetry, if it does not
reverberate) as the melody, the beauty of the word-
music, make

> when the sea-mew
> Flies, as once before it flew,
> O'er thine isles depopulate,
> And all is in its ancient state,
> Save where many a palace gate
> With green sea-flowers overgrown
> Like a rock of ocean's own,
> Topples o'er the abandoned sea,
> As the tides change sullenly,

reverberate; or as

unheard
Save of the quiet Primrose, and the span
Of heaven and few ears

does.

One suspects that some of our contemporaries are a little afraid to be melodious. May they have said, I have thought they may have said, 'Let So-and-so, who thought of nothing else but to be melodious, and ended by being over-sweet, be a warning to us.' Warnings are never of much value to poets; only examples are, good examples. 'If Shakespeare and Keats, and Shelley and Heine, speaking the deep things they had felt, thought it right to speak them melodiously, it must always be right to speak so,'—that is what we should say. Dr. Thompson's last poem is about a tree: he had not, my thought is, desire enough, when writing it, to sing to us; the desire that Horace had, when, in his so different language, he wrote:

. . . neque harum, quas colis, arborum
te praeter invisas cupressos
ulla brevem dominum sequetur.

Another poem of imagery of Dr. Thompson is:

Smoking Reeds
See how the struggling fire
From the damp heap in a white wraith escapes;

But, deep within, the red heart fiercer glows,
Till with a leap the ghost becomes a god,
And shouts and dances on his shrivelling cage.

That is a poem belonging to a group in which there are several. Dr. Thompson has a mind upon which common things, as a fire of reeds, or it might be of dry and withered Yule-tide decorations, or flowers, or bird flights, burn themselves. Because of a mind wedded to his eyes, he sees natural things just as much more to his purpose as a poet, as a clear-eyed painter would see things better to his purpose as a painter, than a short-sighted one. We have all watched a fire, as of reeds, with interest, much as children do; and that we have done it as children do is shown by this, that we see no beginning to a poem about it such as Dr. Thompson has written. To be able to write such poems, a man must be peculiarly *en rapport* with the thing; and when a man is that, he writes a poem that is definitely a new door opened. Study the *Golden Treasury*, and you will find that it falls into groups of poems that are fundamentally the same thing. Shakespeare will write of Youth and Age, and so will Coleridge; Milton will write political sonnets, and so will Wordsworth; there are poems of Wordsworth that bear the relation of cousinship to poems of Vaughan; Byron's and Shelley's poems in praise of women were not fundamentally dis-similar to poems of an earlier day. When Vaughan wrote 'I saw eternity the other night,' he opened a new door, I believe; that is to say, that up to his date no English poet had written anything like it.

One often hears the poetry of our time spoken of slightingly: true, of much of it it may be said that its content are things not significant; but if one were to compile an anthology on the principle that no poem was admitted that did not open a new door, it would be found, I believe, that the largest group was of poems of our day. The anthologist would have to draw on Dr. Thompson's books.

To return to his poem, *Smoking Reeds*—what one misses in it is rhythm, let me think. But here a word. It is my thought that I should not say too much as one appraising; for no contemporary critic should do that. What I hold he should do is to select, with the best of his judgement, from a new man's work, and lay that best before people, not committing himself to more than this: that in his opinion it is work that deserves the study, the frequent readings, that will 'create in us the taste by which to appreciate it.' That is task enough for a contemporary critic, and not to venture more is the recognition required of us by the repeated failures of the critics of the past; a recognition, moreover, required of readers as well as of critics; for if readers will that a critic should appraise, needs must he.

The poem of imagery in Dr. Thompson's work that I think has the strongest claim to such study as I speak of is:

The New Year
Red berries on the banyan !
And in the pipal-tree
The sickle of a silver moon
Most beautiful to see !

Red berries on the holly !
And in the apple-leaves
A waxen gleam of mistletoe,
A rustling stir, a silver glow,
White beard and sickle's glint which show
A Druid ghost of long ago
That gathers in his sheaves !

If that fails of something, it is that it is more fanciful than imaginative, and that the melody again fails of depth: it has not the deeper note of:

In a drear-nighted December,
Too happy, happy tree;

but it is no shock to me to read it either immediately before or immediately after the poem of Keats. Whether in the poem of Dr. Thompson

(Keats was but writing fundamentally the same thing that Shakespeare had written) there is a new door opened is a very deep question.

The following, written at Shumran in Mesopotamia, is a farewell to a country grown familiar to Dr. Thompson during the War, as so many countries to so many men, but never likely to be seen again:

> Red Autumn on the banks,
> Where, thorough fields that bear no grain,
> A desolate Mother treads
> By the brimming river, torn with rain!
> A chill wind moves in the faded ranks
> Of the rushes, rumpling their russet heads.
> And out of the mist, on the racing stream
> As I drift, I know that there gathers fast,
> Over the lands I shall see no more,
> Another mist, which with life shall last,
> Till all that I watched and my comrades bore
> Will be autumn mist, in an old man's dream.

The following is a sad *Nunc Dimittis*, which like the glad one might have been without imagery, but there is imagery in it. The ghost-plowman is such as the foul fiend in the medieval chronicle of Lanercost, a chronicle that had been among Dr. Thompson's reading. The story is that a monastery brought a corrupt action to take away some common rights, and succeeded by means of a bribed jury. The jury one by one sickened and died, 'and during about two years afterwards there appeared in that country a fiery plough, glowing like hot brass, having a most foul fiend as driver, who drove the dead men, harnessed in that manner, to the ground where he had incited them to guile when living'. The poem is:

> O Plowman, thrusting thro' the furze and thistle
> Thy dripping, sanguine share,
> Silent, with onward stare
> Driving, athwart the wintry blasts that whistle,
> Thy furrows that are graves, wherein our best
> Are laid, their tortured, broken limbs at rest!
> I pray thee speak, and say thou dost prepare
> A bed for one, whose eyes, that may not weep,
> Have seen all comrades slain, and buried deep.

Of descriptive poetry, which better suits our earth-loving paces, Dr. Thompson's volumes are full, and it is often so happy that, though the poems do not stir that deepest passion in us that great poetry stirs, they are revelations of the secrets of things. Those that have appealed most to me are:

> *Norton Common*
>
> Flowing at last, now Pix
> Through willowherb's jungle of gray, dry sticks
> Straggles, while thwart-flung twig and grasses
> In flakes of shadow his waves thrust down.

Black-berried privet cowers, drab, forlorn,
And the ragged thorn
Out of all his swelling, crimson crown
Scarce a handful lifts of wrinkled haws.
Flits furtive jay round bushes brown,
And, with sudden rush under briar's red clusters,
Fugitive blackbird flusters.

The Yarmuk Valley

Light green of tamarisk shows
Pale on the dark, sharp oleander-leaves;
Deep through a jungle Yarmuk flows,
With loop and curve his swift path cleaves;
And the long valley glows,
A burnished shield, far-sheeted with gold,
With light packed full as the hills can hold.
Though tamarisk's head 's but a clouded dust,
His beauty faded, his youth grown pale,
Red hollyhocks
Flower from the steep, rough rocks;
Rose-laurels over the oil-black shale
Their fragrant, pink-tipped spears upthrust;
And the reed-muffled brook through the vale
Runs glad, for the Goat-God lies—
Great Pan, whom mosquitoes trouble not,
And who, since a Baal, 's immune from flies—
Piping at ease in some wind-cool grot.

Willian Trees

The winter evening spills
Its store of quietness ineffable,

And from its horn of beauty fills
The empty elms with sunset.
Low fields lie blue in distance; the grove throws
A shadow-copse on the gleaming lake's repose.
Against the darkness glows
One lamp, a diamond.

Damascus Orchards

Lovely with almond-blossom and flooded water
With wind-flushed sheen of swaying orchard-meadows;
With azure starred of infrequent grape-hyacinth;
Misted blue with the fig-groves' wintry haze;
Ruddy with budded apricots; snowy with apple—
Damascus, now into April glory awakening.

The Last Vigil

Under the swaying boughs of the apple,
Where gracious snows drip down,
Knee-deep in early flowers I stand,
Waiting, at watch where the sunbeams dapple
The spring-time, flecking with silver the brown
And emerald, glowing wave-bright on my drawn brand.

The melody, elsewhere somewhat lacking, is in those last three.

There are poems on the East in Dr. Thompson's volumes, and, seeing how rare it is for an Englishman to succeed in grasping the elusive charm of those still lands sufficiently for poetry, and believing that Dr. Thompson has succeeded, I would

like to give several from that group. A later addition to the group, the fruit, I believe, of another
visit to the Near East, was recently published in
The Nation and Athenaeum. I would like to give it,
but I may not, nor any others of that group; but
I will give five poems, choosing them with the
object of showing Dr. Thompson's range (with
what have already been given), that being probably the best way in which to substantiate my
having said that his experience of life, as shown by
his work, has been such as to establish his claim
to be read. (Not that mere reading, as people read
the poetry published in their own day, would be
enough.) I will try to place the poems in such an
order that it, the order, will add something to the
value of the poems. Dr. Thompson's range strikes
me as wider unquestionably than is at all common
among the writers of our day, and that, if it is so,
is again a claim.

The first poem, *Wild Broom*, is perhaps the best
of all. Once, and sufficiently, a thing not done
before, the broom in flower is made to pass into
English poetry. That is to open a door.

Wild Broom

O perishing, wasteful Broom,
Each spur and spire
A splendour outleaping, a flickering fire,

Thou wilt burn thyself out!
Why lavish thy gold
On this bleak hillside where no eyes behold,
Save the flitting birds, that pass unaware,
And the scuttering bunnies who never care?
Be thrifty, and keep for the bare, dark days
Some wisp of bright raiment, some spark of thy blaze !
Be wiser, O Broom !
Be wastrel no longer, but mindful of doom !

But the Broom—
I flame, I expire;
I am Beauty's plumage, my wings are a fire;
For a boon, neither buying nor sold,
I scatter my gold.
I have made this hillside one far-trumpeted shout.
Sky and field may behold,
And the wind-ragged rout
Of tumultuous clouds,
The passionate dawn, and the hurrying crowds
Of fear-stricken lives, they may pause, they may listen
To my pealing thanksgiving,
My clamouring glory, my fierce boughs that glisten,
And blaze to dry scrub, as I perish by living. . . .
Your chaffer I flout,
Your marts and your pricings, your wisdom I scout.
But, oh, the mad joy as I burn myself out !

Epilogue

With words as counters, talk of day and night,
Sun, moon and stars, using such toys as these,

I play, who towards the timeless shape my flight,
Seeking a home that knows nor lands nor seas.
Hereafter, on the mirror of that mind,
If any shadow of these times should fall,
Amid that brighter world how shall I find
Utterance that can my vanished dreams recall—
How magical the orange moon arose
Over my palms or on stark Moab hills;
How musical the brook of Weston flows
Through hazel shade which March with windflowers fills?
So, after sleep, its mists of fleeing thought
Vainly upon the mind's clear sky are sought.

The Visit

I stood with chalk in hand, at point to trace
Hard meanings on the board,
When suddenly His face
Shone in—abstracted, sad, as though He sought
Within that frequence something, finding nought
Of all He hoped for, marking there alone
One long a slave, unprofitable known.

Dear disappointed Presence, come again!
For though, with vision foiled and failing brain,
I falter from the gracious duty set,
I could be faithful, did the Face remain,
I could remember, didst not Thou forget.
And, Soul, be swift and eager, that, when next
The room grows calm beneath thy gazing Lord,

Those eyes may rest, with no misgiving vexed,
Well-pleased upon thee where thou dost fufil
With gleaming chalk and ignorant lips His will !

F. B.

She dwells within the temple of my heart,
A little priestess; her remembered face
A silence makes in that dishallowed place,
A silence whence a nobler song shall start.
The walls that sin's fierce anger rent apart
Lo ! vines she planted bind and interlace,
A shelter making and a chequered space,
By shadow and sunshine woven with gracious art.

Dear child, if you inhabit still this fane,
I think it will become God's home again;
The Dove will brood within the shattered shrine;
There will be altar both, and mercyseat;
And in the place a little child made sweet
Heaven's peace upon a kneeling man will shine.

The Owl and the Lady

Owl in the hollybush
Sitting so still,
With wide eyes staring—
What Fear climbs the hill? . .

Now, through the winter eve
Tinted with flame,
Riding, a Lady
Along the wood came. . . .

If the bird were a man,
He would leap for the sight,
But the foolish old owl
Is already in flight!

On the pale, flushing skies,
To wet fields he flits down,
And is lost, as he settles,
Brown wings in the brown.

PUBLISHING LYRICAL
POETRY

THERE is an ease for a man in the presence of children, the ease of being with those who are themselves irresponsible and innocent, and who assume that others are too, even a man with grey hair. That has always been for me the greatest attraction of children of which I could give a reasonable account. They have an attraction, and little girls have especially, that I cannot give a reasonable account of. On that side they stir me, not merely down to my feet, but, as I feel it, through half a dozen past and buried lives. If the presence of irresponsible creatures is always a relief to me, it has been so specially during the last few weeks; for I have done a thing that makes me feel, among older persons, like a doomed soul: I have published a volume of lyrical poetry. The writing of such a volume is a great experience for the spirit of men, and one that a man would not consent to miss; but the man who can publish such a thing without shrinking from the sight of it, when the book first appears and for long afterwards, is one that I have difficulty in understanding. There should be for the writer's ease an

interval of fifty years between his poems appearing
in print and his seeing them in anybody's hands.

We think of Shelley as a poet, and, however
from his soul's soul his utterance may be, to us it
seems right; it is what we expect; those poems are
those that we have got by heart, and the poems
that we recite when the talk is of Shelley. But then
for us there is a cloud round Shelley, the man: the
man lives for us in a remoteness as of a desert.
But suppose we know Shelley as a man who might
any day be seen going to the baker's to pay for last
month's bread; as a man making arrangements
with an ostler for riding horses; as a man well
dressed or in shabby clothes; one who shaves
every day, or occasionally 'forgets'; as a man,
finally, who writes poetry, but we do not know
that. Then suppose that one day we take up a new
book, and, opening it, find his name on the title-
page, and, turning over the pages, come upon
such a poem as this:

> One word is too often profaned
>   For me to profane it,
> One feeling too falsely disdained
>   For thee to disdain it.
> One hope is too like despair
>   For prudence to smother,
> And pity from thee more dear
>   Than love from another.

I can give not what men call love;
But wilt thou accept not
The worship the heart lifts above
And the Heavens reject not;
The desire of the moth for the star,
Of the night for the morrow,
The devotion to something afar
From the sphere of our sorrow.

Suppose men come suddenly upon such a poem as that, in the book of a neighbour they know well. The less worthy of them will ask whom this man is addressing such words to: whom—fie, for shame—he has fallen so much in love with. So the less worthy. The more worthy will be so much impressed by the beauty of the poetry, as not to want to ask questions. Now think of Shelley himself. He knew himself as thought of by his neighbours yesterday only as a man who might any day be seen talking to the baker or the ostler; thought of as one who paid his debts; thought of as dressing well or shabbily. Now he must see himself as one they know, those of them who have read his poem, for a man who has had an experience; who has thought of it, not vulgarly, but with that tenderness; who did not press forward and grasp more, as a vulgar man would have done, but turned aside to make that purity of poetry about it, and

as now offering the poetry to mankind as a thing
that, let mankind love it, will make it purer; as offering it in the same spirit in which he offers what is
to be read on another page of his book; this:

> Be through my lips to unawakened earth
> The trumpet of a prophecy.

Now follow me, please, a little farther in my
attempt to present Shelley, the man, as one in
whose thought is uppermost the knowledge that
he is now, for the first time, visible to his neighbours, all the coarse, all the refined, with the
recesses opened of a more than usually sensitive
soul; for without such a soul, how could he write
such lyrics? What I want you to see is the storm
of shyness, bashfulness, what the French mean by
pudeur, that must fill the Shelley heart. I want
you to see that, that I may have the same ease with
you as with irresponsible, innocent-feeling children; so that I may lose the sense of being a doomed
soul that the sight of my book in the hands of any
of my neighbours gives me. I write about all this,
that you may understand a man's feelings; also
because there is an interest in the subject apart
from you, apart from me, and I do not remember
any piece of writing in which that interest is
explored.

No man makes a poem like the one of Shelley's

that I have quoted except out of the stuff of an experience lived through; not one merely imagined; not that the subject-matter is beyond the reach of the imagination, but the passion of the poem is the passion of actual experience. Had Shelley shunned the experience, we should not have the poem. I should like to ask him a question; this one: 'Did you deliberately seek such experiences, having discovered that there was lyrical poetry to be made out of such stuff better far than any other man's lyrics; those of that other man's, that is, that were not made, each of the stuff of such another experience, whether sought or come unsought, but were things imagined?' If Shelley should answer that he did, and would again, if life were to come over again, it would not be for me to blame him, for I have done it myself. (There, I have told you.) There are hundreds of things involved in that; for, if Shelley and I are right, then you are all of you wrong: the basis that you have all been taught to accept as the basis of the finest life is seen to be not the right one. For if you do not write, all or any of you, each his poem, you have got to live one. So the Shelley way should be yours also.

In an eighteenth-century poem on the sugar-cane were the words, 'O Muse, let's sing of mice.' (The manuscript was read aloud to Dr. Johnson.)

That is the kind of stuff (it may not be all as bad as that; there may be a little of the breath of God, breathed into the dust, in some of it) that a man will find himself writing, if he attempts to make poetry out of the stores of his intellect. They did that in the eighteenth century: we should be doing it still but for Blake, Wordsworth, Keats, and others. Even a man of as late a date as Macaulay's —it was Macaulay himself—could suggest the river Thames as a very good subject for a poem. So it would be—in a world fallen into decrepit age. There would be nothing in it, either for sense or rhythm, to compare with:

> One word is too often profaned
> For me to profane it.

There would be nothing remotely like:

> Be through my lips to unawakened earth
> The trumpet of a prophecy.

The men who would not choose the river Thames or the sugar-cane as the subjects of their poems would lead different lives from those led by the men who would choose such subjects, and the great question for the world to answer (it has not yet done so: it is a great mistake to think that it has, and that the matter has been settled against Shelley) is this one: Were those men's lives just so

much better than the other men's as their poetry
was better than the other men's poetry? Shelley's
poetry lives; one might say that it is more alive
now than it was a hundred years ago. The poem
on the sugar-cane has died a new death every day
for more than a hundred years now, and by that
you may judge how dead it is. It is ten thousand
times dead. It might be reprinted; anything may
be reprinted.

It would be an odd thing surely, to go back to
the author of the poem on the sugar-cane, if his
way of living should be really and truly a better
thing than Shelley's way. If it was a worse thing,
then that concerns us; for we have all been taught
to follow that way. I assure you it is so: there is
far more of the way of thinking of the author of
the poem on the sugar-cane in the copybooks than
there is of Shelley's way. In fact, there is not
a single syllable of Shelley's way from beginning
to end of the copybooks.

The same onward movement, irresistible as
a tide of the sea, or as planetary motion, that carried the generation of Coleridge and Shelley so
far from Dr. Johnson and his sugar-cane friend
—that same onward-moving force has carried us
a long way from Shelley. Shelley just might have
chosen the river Thames as the subject of a poem:

Keats did choose subjects out of books. Impossible, that, for us: the only things that we can write poetry about are the experiences of our own lives; or, at least, the poetry that we write that has part of that experience for its subject is the only part that we can think of as being read a hundred years hence.

You will understand that when I speak of a man's life-experience as the stuff for his poetry, I mean the whole of it that was charged enough with feeling. That is, I mean a very big thing. The Oxford Movement entered into my father's experience, and I think of the Church of England as having entered mine; but if the Oxford Movement had not stirred my father more than to an inch below his skin, nor me the Church of England, then of neither could we have made poetry. But had it fallen to me to be bootblack in a big hotel, and black boots all day and part of the night, and had I hated it enough, then I might have made a poem out of that. Or had I, poor bootblack, got out into the country once in a blue moon; if I had loved that enough, I could have made poetry of it. And if a beautiful princess had put up in the hotel, and one more than just beautiful in face and figure; had I had a sharp enough sense of her, I might have made a poem about her like one of Shelley's.

That as a parenthesis. To go back. The onward-moving force, as I have said, the force irresistible as a tide of the sea or as planetary motion, has carried us as far from Shelley as it had carried Shelley from the sugar-cane man, and in the same direction. That is, towards making our poetry out of the most intimate experiences of our lives. So that, if it must have been a shock to Shelley (I do not know for certain that it was; you never can be certain how any man will feel about anything) to think of himself as now at last seen by his neighbours as naked, it must be so much more a shock to us, that we show ourselves as so much more naked. Which makes the publication of a volume of lyrical poetry a horrible experience, and that was all that I wanted to say.

IN CONCLUSION

A REVIEWER of a new biography of Shelley had:

'What is too little flown at in Mr. Peck's biography, the secret and the talisman, is at all events for ever young, fine and ready to renew its enchantment in Shelley's poems; there is the spirit beautiful and swift, with its convocation of all the clearest light, sound and motion that humanity was ever able to conceive, its pageantry of Eden and Olympus, of azure Italy and worlds and worlds in the divine abyss. Here Pan's sweet pipings make a silence, save for the low concent of liquid Peneus, hard by the haunt of the moonlight-coloured may, the wild roses and ivy serpentine. There is no repeating and recounting these beauties, these symbols of Shelley's essential life, without a strengthened persuasion that the poet who spent his short years so laboriously in attempting the impossible by this world's reckoning was indeed an intelligence apart, Orphic, beyond our measure; this music, flowing free as a fountain, has witchcraft in it, and defies locality.

A ship is floating in the harbour now,
A wind is hovering o'er the mountain's brow;
There is a path on the sea's azure floor,
No keel has ever ploughed that path before.

Such magic would retain its power however casually or drably the verse were committed to paper . . .'

I do not feel quite sure whether the magic that

the critic speaks of, or was thinking of, if it is to be found in the poetry of Shelley's writing, which no one doubts, is also to be found in the four lines quoted. There is no magic in those four lines: they are very childish. Just such lines any poet-boy might be found writing at school at, say, twelve years of age. 'A ship is floating in the harbour now'—yes, that is well within the reach of a boy poet. 'What rhymes with "now"?' he would then say;—'yes, "brow," ' and he would soon have, 'A wind is hovering o'er the mountain's brow.' 'Sea's azure floor'—those were words in common enough currency, when I was a boy at school. I can remember using them myself when I was ten years old, before I had read any Shelley or Byron. They were in the loose air I breathed with the other boys. I do not know in what poem of Shelley's the four lines come, but only that, if it is all like the four, the poem should have been burnt.

The question one would like answered, is how a man, obviously so deep in Shelley, could think the four lines worth quoting. It was a lapse? It is stupid of me to dwell on it? I think it is not stupid: I see it as no lapse. If there is, as Professor Garrod has said, a great deal of poetry not worth reading, there will as certainly be a great deal of writing about poetry that is not worth reading.

One could make one's account with some, even
with a great deal: yes, so much was to be expected
not to be worth reading. But when it comes, as
more and more it appears, to hardly any of it being
worth reading; when one may be confronted with
fine critics, even the finest, who are at their ease as
long as they are dealing with prose, but feel, when
it is a poem, and show it plainly, that it is a world
beyond them—then one may ask how it should be
so. Dr. Johnson, as a critic of poetry, could be put
beside his part by any prejudice; he was not to be
held back, by any sense that he was dealing with
a high matter, from what would have made him
say, had another written it, 'He lies, and he knows
he lies.' Did Sir Leslie Stephen, that fine critic of
prose, see his way clearly in poetry? One thinks
not. Does Professor Saintsbury see his? Is it
possible that the power to tell great poetry from
lesser, never to fail of that judgement, is a gift
almost as seldom bestowed as the gift to write
great poetry? Do men generally take on trust from
others that the poetry of Shakespeare, Milton,
Keats is in a class apart, not really themselves
knowing what makes it so? There is evidence
that they do.

The gravest error that men make in their judgements of poetry is such an error as they make in

disregarding or dismissing the two great opinions of Shelley's poetry, Keats's and Arnold's. When Keats wrote, urging Shelley to load every rift with ore, he judged his poetry: if he had not seen that Shelley did not load every rift with ore, he would have said something else. Arnold's judgement is well known, but I will give it again in full.

'These great poets unite in themselves the faculty of both kinds of interpretation, the naturalistic and the moral. But it is observable that in the poets who unite both kinds, the latter (the moral) usually ends by making itself the master. In Shakespeare the two kinds seem wonderfully to balance one another; but even in him the balance leans; his expression tends to become too little sensuous and simple, too much intellectualized. The same thing may be yet more strongly affirmed of Lucretius and of Wordsworth. In Shelley there is not a balance of the two gifts, nor even a co-existence of them, but there is a passionate striving after them both, and this is what makes Shelley, as a man, so interesting. I will not now inquire how much Shelley achieves as a poet, but whatever he achieves, he in general fails to achieve natural magic in his expression; in Mr. Palgrave's charming *Treasury* may be seen a gallery of his failures.'

And in a foot-note:

'Compare, for example, his "Lines Written in the Euganean Hills" with Keats's "Ode to Autumn". The latter piece *renders* Nature; the former *tries to render* her. I will not deny, however, that Shelley has natural magic in his rhythm; what I deny is, that he has it in his language. It always seems to me that the right sphere for Shelley's genius was the sphere of music, not of poetry; the medium of sounds he can master, but to master the more difficult medium of words he has neither intellectual force enough nor sanity enough.'

One reads, I did only the other day, that 'Arnold had a mind to which Shelley's poetry did not appeal'. With such words men dismiss the judgement. That will not do. What Arnold says is true. He was the man with probably the deepest insight into the facts of poetry of any Englishman there has ever been. When he delivered a careful, reasoned judgement on any question of English poetry, he spoke a thing he knew. It is thirty years and more now since I first read Arnold's judgement of Shelley. Never since have I quite ceased to think of it, and there have been times when I have gone again, step by step, through the argument and the evidence it rests on. It was worth it: it is a judgement, not of Shelley only, but of all poets and of poetry. If any man, I say, cannot see how much greater the *Ode to Autumn* is than Shelley's *Lines*, rather, that the *Ode* is great poetry, while the *Lines* are not, then I say that he is no judge. If any one has not seen the lack of

sanity and intellectual force in Shelley's poetry,
let him read Shelley's letters again. Arnold is right
in every word he says. It is not true that he had a
mind to which Shelley's poetry did not appeal.
His mind was one to which Shelley's poetry, so
far as it is poetry, did appeal: he only saw, clear-
eyed man that he was, the point where it fails and
ends. The men to whom Shelley's poetry appeals
more than Keats's does, for there are many such,
are men without understanding of the highest
poetry; and you will find them preferring other
poets whom they should not prefer, and admiring
other poetry more than it deserves to be admired.
Arnold could not be put beside his part by any
prejudice, egotism, or preference; he was under
a divine compulsion to tell the truth about poetry.
He felt an unerring sense for poetry to be the
greatest good that a man could possess, and I
believe he was right.

Mr. Fausset, in the Preface to his 'Studies in
Idealism', has, 'There is scarcely a superlatively
great poem in the world to which mankind was
emotionally true enough to respond immediately.'
True enough or *old* enough? It is not an idle
question; for, if mankind was not emotionally old
enough to respond to the poem, at the time it was
written, and if to-day it is emotionally no older,

not a day, it is still too young to respond. I do not believe that mankind was emotionally not true enough, but, in the course of some fifty years, say, grew emotionally true enough for the particular poem; if a man grows emotionally true enough for one poem, he grows so for all poetry, and that is what mankind has never been. After fifty years or so mankind is where it was, but by that time one or two men, speaking with authority, will have spoken for the new poem, and the race will have accepted the poem; but so much as was beyond its emotional reach will still lie beyond it. Dr. Johnson could write of *Lycidas* as he did, with no fear of the whole country rising up and saying, 'But we all know better than that.' The man who said it would take an Act of Parliament to make one read Shakespeare's sonnets felt safe from contradiction.

The importance of a hard study of poetry, but under the guidance of such men as Arnold, for all the best of it lies beyond the common man's own reach, and the fatal thing is to imagine that, if you prefer Shelley, say, or Francis Thompson, or Burns, to Shakespeare and Milton, you cannot do better than read Shelley, when you could do better, and, if you are to grow older, must do better—the importance of a hard study of poetry, I say, is that therein lies more hope for the emotional growth of mankind than in any other direction that one can see. Men do not apparently grow emotionally ᴧr psychologically any older for all their study of natural science, or any other branch of logic: mankind's youthfulness is in its emotional nature, and so, if by study it is to grow older, it must be by study of what is concerned with that nature. On mankind's growth lies its highest hope for the future.